A John Catt Publication

THE THIRTY YEARS WAR

MY LIFE REPORTING ON EDUCATION

RICHARD GARNER

First Published 2016

by John Catt Educational Ltd,
12 Deben Mill Business Centre, Old Maltings Approach,
Melton, Woodbridge IP12 1BL

Tel: +44 (0) 1394 389850 Fax: +44 (0) 1394 386893
Email: enquiries@johncatt.com
Website: www.johncatt.com

ISBN: 978 1 911 382 058

Set and designed by John Catt Educational Limited

Contents

Prologue...5

Chapter One – Thatcher: The Early Years................................9

Chapter Two – Trouble and Strife.......................................25

Chapter Three – The Day of the GERBIL 38

Chapter Four – The Major Years...53

Chapter Five – Education, education, education....................68

Chapter Six – "I was Charming. He was Offensive"................83

Chapter Seven – Going. Going. Gove....................................97

Chapter Eight – And now for something completely different
... Education, education, education 112

Chapter Nine – After the Lord Mayor's Show 128

Epilogue 143

Prologue

I can remember it almost as if it was yesterday. I was driving down from Birmingham – where I had been living and working for the *Birmingham Evening Mail* – to London where I was taking up a new job with the *Times Educational Supplement* (or *TES* as it is now universally known). I reached to switch the car radio on. It was always tuned in to Radio One in those days and it wasn't long before the number one record that week came on – Pink Floyd's 'Another Brick In The Wall' with its famous chorus line "We Don't Need No Education". I remember thinking: I hope they're wrong.

The record, of course, caused quite a storm in the education world. The backing singing was provided by pupils from Islington Green school and Conservatives on the Inner London Education Authority complained that it was wrong that children should be exposed to such anarchic thoughts. However, Trevor Phillips, then chairman of the Equal Opportunities Commission and a former president of the National Union of Students, thought it struck a chord with some young people. Schools, he said, could alienate the young – a point the record was trying to make.

Of course, that car journey wasn't just yesterday. It was 36 years ago – the time when I first started reporting on the national education scene. As I reflect on 36 years of coverage, I do think that record's chant "We Don't Need No Education" (I remember Trevor Averre-Beeson, a one-time headteacher at Islington Green, telling me he tried to convince the pupils that the chant was a double negative and so therefore meant they did need some education – I don't think it worked!) could almost be an anthem for white working class boys in the UK who, statistics tell us, are the worst-performing ethnic group in the country. In many cases, their parents were failed by our education system and therefore do not see it as the route out of poverty and disadvantage that parents from ethnic minority groups – who may have fled as refugees from oppressive regimes – do.

I had mugged up on the problems in our education system before taking up the job on the *TES*. In the week before I joined – the first full working week of the new 80s decade – the main news had been about school library services being wiped out by cuts in public spending, a situation that was causing the School Library Association 'grave concern'. Ironic then that the final story I was to write – for the *i* newspaper in April 2016 – should be about the Association of Teachers and Lecturers bemoaning the fact that one in five schools had cut the service in the past year. Oh, and for good measure, the other main story that week was about a shortage of language skills in the UK. It was a theme I was to return to many a time during my working life as an education journalist and was to bring me my biggest 'scoop' – an interview with the German, Italian and Spanish ambassadors bemoaning the fact that Labour had just scrapped compulsory language lessons for 14 to 16-year-olds, a decision I believe to this day to have been one of the worst made during its period of office from 1997 to 2010. Sadly, many a time during my 36 years I seem to have been reporting on surveys which showed the UK to be the 'language dunces of Europe' with the lowest number of pupils opting to take the subject at GCSE and A-level.

So what had brought me to the job on the *TES*? How had I managed to convince them that they should employ me? I think the crucial meeting had been in a pub (much journalistic work was done those days in such institutions) with Lucy Hodges, then news editor of the *TES*. The paper had not been published for a year due to the lock-out of the print workers at *The Times* but was returning to publication. The problem was a number of its staff had resigned – finding new jobs – during the dispute and it needed to find new education writers in a hurry. As luck would have it, Lucy decided to ring her brother-in-law, Tom McGhie, who worked alongside me at the *Post and Mail*. He told her there was a chap who had reported on education while working in head office but was now covering general news during a stint in the London office. Would I be interested, he asked me. Yes, I replied. Hence the setting up of the pub meeting – and, ultimately, the offer of a job.

Ironically, I had applied to the *TES* before but was turned down on the grounds they didn't employ non-graduates (I was probably unique in my experience of the education world on the *TES* having not set foot in a state school after the age of seven and having not been to university). I did, however, have experience of the further education sector – something not many journalists today can claim

– through a National Council for the Training of Journalists course at what was then known as Harlow Technical College. Needs must, though, from the *TES's* point of view, and so that was why I found myself entering the *Times* building (they shared the same offices in these days) in Grays Inn Road as an employee on Monday, January 7, 1980.

What did I know about the education system back then? Well, during the 18 months I had covered the subject in Birmingham the main news focus had been on the teachers' pay dispute in 1978 when they withdrew from midday supervision in support of their salaries claim. It had a devastating effect in Birmingham with pupils leaving the premises during their lunch break and – in some cases – running riot in the city. I can remember that in those days schools could still use the cane as a punishment and it was wielded regularly during that dispute – even, in one case, on girls. That stuck in my mind, and if I am to reflect on what was the most important advance in the education system during my 36 years of reporting, I would have to say the abolition of corporal punishment would rank highly.

There was also the controversy over selection. Birmingham has always retained selective state schools – the five grammar schools of the King Edward's Foundation – and I can recall Shirley Williams, then Labour's Education Secretary, arriving at the NUT annual conference in 1978 promising to take action to compel the schools to become comprehensive. It never happened and, in the latter years of my working life, I reported on how the Foundation is making great strides in trying to counter one of the most relevant criticisms of the grammar school system: that it only takes in a handful of disadvantaged pupils. Their parents, obviously, cannot afford the extra tutoring and coaching that the middle classes go in for to ensure their children pass the 11-plus. The Foundation now offers places to those entitled to free school meals on a lower score in the 11-plus – a practice now being copied by others of England's 164 remaining grammar schools. If I pass on one thought for my successors as education journalists, it would be this: see how these pupils fare at GCSE compared with their richer classmates. The results could be fascinating.

I should perhaps add here that I am still opposed to the 11-plus as it is an iniquitous way of determining school admissions. It is just that I am a realist: Labour has been in power for 26 years of my life and has never got round to completely eradicating selection. It doesn't even seem top of a Jeremy Corbyn-led party's wish list. If we are to have grammar schools, it is right they should offer a route out of poverty for the most disadvantaged students.

As I prepared to write this book, though, I recalled a third event during my time in Birmingham. Before my time, in October 1976 actually, then Prime Minister Jim Callaghan made a speech at Ruskin College in which he launched what he termed a 'great debate' on the future of education. My first job as an education reporter on the *Birmingham Evening Mail* was to go and cover one of the consultation conferences – in Solihull – which stemmed from that speech. Callaghan's speech was the start of the closer involvement of politicians in determining the future shape of the education system. Their encroachment has been fought tooth and nail by most of the teachers' organisations over the years. Before Callaghan's speech, there was no national curriculum, schools did not have to publish their exam results, all state schools were maintained by the local education authority, and the inspectorate – HMI – did not publish reports on individual schools. The curriculum was often referred to as a 'secret garden'. All that was to change over the 36 years I was in post and is still changing. Hence the title of this book – *The Thirty Years War.* Except it is more than 30 years now.

Chapter One
Thatcher: The Early Years

I doubt whether the mention of the name of Mark Carlisle in education circles would bring back floods of memories about radical changes to the education system, yet he held the post of Education Secretary as I started my career in writing about the national education scene. He had not been a high flyer in Conservative circles in the days before the Thatcher government came to power. Indeed, there were those who said that his appointment indicated the relative priority that Mrs Thatcher was planning to give education in her first term, *ie* not that high. If anything, he was on the 'wet' side of her cabinet in the days when those who felt she was going too far too fast were so described. That may not have been an accurate assessment, though. He was certainly no critic of her economic policies. It may just have been that, as head of a spending department, he was often having to fight his own corner by going cap in hand to the government to plead for more public spending on education.

At the beginning of 1980, he was concentrating on a couple of policy initiatives which were to loom large in the years and even decades ahead. The first was a consultation over a framework for the curriculum which had been started the previous November. The government's intention was to lay down the amount of time that should be set aside for core areas of the curriculum – the document suggested 10 per cent for maths and English and between 10 per cent and 20 per cent for science and modern foreign languages. It was, if you like, a forerunner of the National Curriculum – but more modest in its aim. The consultation document suggested that these aims should be adhered to for at least the first two years of secondary schooling.

It may have been modest in its aims but it still incurred the wrath of the teachers' organisations. Up until 1980, the curriculum had been regarded as a 'secret garden' and there was still a feeling abound that it was best left up to teachers to decide what should be taught in the classroom. Gradually, the proposals were watered down, with ministers saying after the consultation period that they were merely designed to influence what schools should be teaching – and there should be no statutory force behind them. Eventually, in March 1981, the call for minimum amounts of time for core subjects was dropped altogether on the grounds that the proposals had failed to find enough agreement on them. It was not the kind of argument that would have won the day 30 years later when then Education Secretary Michael Gove was publishing details of his school reforms (indeed, he would have relished taking his opponents on) – or even later that same decade when Kenneth Baker set about reforming the state education system. The revamped document simply sought to persuade schools to make every effort to ensure their pupils did not drop vital subject areas during compulsory secondary schooling. "This paper has a very different status from the one we published a year ago," admitted Carlisle. The general reaction from teachers' organisations was that the final draft was 'unexceptional'.

The second item in Mark Carlisle's in-tray at the beginning of that year was paving the way for the introduction of the Assisted Places Scheme – whereby bright children from poorer homes could get cash aid to take up places at independent schools. It was due to come into force in 1981 and eventually provide places for between 80,000 and 100,000 children. There was already opposition to the idea in cabinet with at least two ministers considering it to be an 'electoral albatross' – unpopular in the education world and 'inappropriate' at a time when the sector was having to face considerable cuts in spending. Nevertheless, the government did go ahead with the scheme. It was repealed when Labour came into power in 1997. Critics had claimed that it had not managed to target the most disadvantaged. Instead, it favoured the children of those parents who knew how to play the system. Many of those who benefited from it were the children of teachers, for instance.

A third item which made its first appearance on the political agenda early in 1980 was a proposal for the break up of the Inner London Education Authority – drafted by a policy group called 'Sherlock' chaired by Kenneth Baker, a politician who was to have considerable influence on the education system over the next 30 years. (It was called 'Sherlock' because Baker Street is where Sherlock Holmes lives. Geddit?) It proposed either abolishing the authority – usually Labour led with quite a radical approach to policy – but with a minority of Conservative-controlled councils, Kensington and Chelsea, Westminster and

Wandsworth. It took Mr Baker inheriting the job of Secretary of State before the plan came to fruition – with the ILEA first becoming directly elected and then being abolished with responsibility being transferred to the individual inner London boroughs.

That, then, was the agenda I was confronted with.

*****

My first task on reporting for duty at the *TES* was to look into the Clegg Commission on teachers' pay and try and find out as much as I could about what it was planning to offer the profession. It had been set up in the dying days of the Callaghan government as a means of overcoming industrial unrest in schools. It would be a fair bet that the Commission would not have been Mrs Thatcher's preferred option for dealing with the problem. To her eyes, it would have been bound to produce an inflationary solution to the problem – thus presenting her with a problem as she tried to control (and limit) public spending.

The teachers' big pay award, of course, was back in 1974 with the report of the Houghton committee of inquiry. It is often said that the announcement of the Houghton award was like a 'JFK moment' for the teaching profession – everyone can remember where they were when they first heard the announcement. I can give some credence to this theory. At the time I was relishing in the title of Municipal Correspondent for the *Kent Evening Post* (local government correspondent really – which meant some coverage of education issues). It was my day off and I was in the bath with my transistor radio on when I heard it on the news. So be it – but another measure of the importance of that day and that award was that for years after that the teachers' unions demanded that their pay levels should be restored to the level set by the Houghton award.

I had spent some time whilst on the *Birmingham Evening Mail* as their education correspondent. It wasn't an exclusive brief. During my spell with that title, I covered various events like the trial of former Liberal party leader Jeremy Thorpe on an attempted murder charge, the assassination of the British Ambassador to the Netherlands by the IRA, and I interviewed Tina Turner on a chaise longue at the Hilton Hotel. (That is still one of my favourite moments. No amount of interviews with Education Secretaries or teachers' union leaders in latter years seem to have capped it!)

I digress. (Somehow I can't get that interview out of my mind – and the after-the-show party that she invited me to.) What I meant to point out was that I had picked up some useful contacts in the education world during that spell and set about asking them what kind of direction the Commission was taking on teachers' pay. The steer they had got was that during an earlier inquiry into nurses' pay Clegg had sought to give bigger rewards to those with more responsibility, *ie* ward sisters got more than nurses. It seemed a fair bet his Commission would take the same line with the teaching profession and that headteachers were likely to get a bigger pay rise than ordinary classroom teachers. I made that the theme of what turned out to be my first front page lead on education for a national paper. In the end, it turned out to be correct with the Commission recommending increases of between 17 per cent and 25 per cent for the profession with the biggest rises going to heads.

Mrs Thatcher had made it clear the government would accept the Clegg award – and the teachers' organisations largely took a similar position. One fear was that the size of the award would lead to local education authorities cutting teachers' jobs to pay for it – something that Fred Jarvis, general secretary of the NUT, said was "not on". The award left teachers five per cent short of the level set by the Houghton award – although I guess today's teachers, brought up on a diet of pay rises limited to one per cent by spending squeezes over the last six years, would salivate at the thought of such a massive rise.

That was not an end to the matter, though. The Commission was forced to admit it had got its sums wrong when comparing teachers' pay to that of other graduates. The award was four percentage points too high – and should have been between 13 per cent and 21 per cent. The Commission put out a statement saying its members "greatly regret that an error of this kind was made". Thatcher more than greatly regretted it and set up an inquiry to find out how the error had occurred. It was said to have emerged during a telephone call made either to the management secretariat of the Burnham committee (the body responsible for determining teachers' pay) or the Department of Education and Science – as it was then called. Legal advice, however, was that the recommendations of the original report were still binding and so therefore had to be paid. Local education authorities again warned that they would deduct the money from the next settlement which ironically was already due as Clegg had been set up in response to the 1979 pay claim.

So the decade had begun with a wrangle over teachers' pay – an issue which was to dominate much of the 1980s in education. It would probably be a fair assumption that it took up a lot of time which the Conservative government would have liked to have spent on developing other reforms to the education system – the reforms which, we shall see, led to increasing control over what was taught in schools and how schools were run being wielded by the government.

*****

Soon after my arrival at the *TES*, I was given the specialist brief of covering the teachers' organisations. All *TES* reporters were specialists within a specialism and I guess that the 'labour relations' brief was – together with the political reporter's job – one of the most sought-after on the paper. Certainly, at a time of cuts and strife over pay, it was one of the high-profile jobs on the paper.

I had dabbled with the idea of moving into political reporting myself at one stage but, on reflection, I am glad I stayed with education. At least in that brief I could meet ordinary people going about their daily lives – rather than live inside the Westminster bubble, listening to the latest conspiracy theory being hatched by MPs.

The cuts threw up their fair share of ordinary people battling against the odds. One such person was Eileen Crosbie, a nursery teacher from Nottingham, who refused to teach her nursery unit of more than 40 children after her nursery assistant had been withdrawn because of the cuts. She considered it was an unsafe environment to be teaching in – but the response of the Nottinghamshire education authority was to suspend and then sack her from her job (on a four to three vote at a disciplinary hearing). Perhaps not surprisingly, the decision provoked strike action by her fellow teachers in a bid to get her job back. Perhaps also unsurprisingly, she was given a heroine's welcome when she appeared at the annual conference of her union, the NUT, that Easter.

Eileen Crosbie's stance won her admiration from more than just the usual suspects. In particular, I remember my colleague John Izbicki rallying to her support in his column in the *Daily Telegraph*. In the end, she was reinstated – but it took over a year and a Labour victory in the county council elections in 1981 before that happened.

Meanwhile, the impact of the cuts rumbled on – and was partly responsible for me witnessing the rough ride given to an Education Secretary at the NUT's Easter conference. Mark Carlisle took the brave decision to tough it out with the teachers. He was given a rowdy reception. Placards were unfurled proclaiming "Smash Tory Cuts", "All Out on May 14" – a reference to a day of action which had been called by the TUC – and "Give Avon Back Its Teachers" (Avon was one of the authorities cutting back on teaching posts). In addition, a total of 111 teachers walked out of his speech in protest. The figure was collated by the NUT itself and showed the fragile relations which existed between the then dominant group on the union's executive (later to be known as the 'broad left' – a sort of left-centre Kinnockite grouping) and the harder left. Responding to accusations that collating the figures was an attempt to discredit those who had walked out, Peter Kennedy, the union's president, said: "It is not an attempt to discredit the left. They have surely discredited themselves." He was equally condemnatory, though, in his assessment of Mr Carlisle, telling him: "We believe that the government has got the priority of education wrong. Because children only get one school life, we are very much aware that we cannot let a whole generation of children come through the maintained system with a cutback in education, which, in my view and the view of this union, was not adequate in the first place." What happened to Mr Carlisle marked a watershed in relations between the NUT and the Conservative government. The following year, rather than address the NUT conference, he took a holiday in Mexico. His successors – Sir Keith Joseph, Kenneth Baker, John MacGregor, Kenneth Clarke and Gillian Shephard – never attended the conference.

The cuts, though, continued and made an impact on parents' pockets. A survey (by the *TES*) of 372 schools in Suffolk showed that parents were forking out around £23 million a year to prop up their schools, assuming the figure was representative of the country as a whole. Mark Carlisle had his say on the subject at the National Association of Head Teachers conference: "Parents can buy books," he said. "I am not for a moment suggesting charging for education. That seems to be totally different from giving encouragement to Parent-Teacher Associations to provide facilities in schools ... There is a limit to what the taxpayer can provide." However, David Hart, the association's general secretary, responded: "The mind boggles at delineating schools as rich or poor and our members would be horrified at that." Eventually, the issue of what schools could and could not charge for was taken up by Kenneth Baker's Great Education Reform Bill – or GERBIL as it became known. They could charge for activities outside of school time provided that they were not a necessary part of the curriculum. One of the thorny issues, though, was over music provision – where there were claims that disadvantaged pupils were being denied the opportunity to take part in after school lessons because of the cost.

*****

Come the summer of 1980 and a new figure emerged on the teachers' union scene. (Actually, some would query whether he was actually a part of the scene as he represented the Professional Association of Teachers – now renamed VOICE – which pledged never to take strike action and, indeed, in one local authority, was only granted recognition by being awarded a seat on the management side in negotiations.)

Step forward Peter Dawson, formerly the headmaster of Eltham Green School in south London, whom John Cleese based his character on in the film, *Clockwise*. He was a strict disciplinarian as a headteacher and his book recalling his experiences at Eltham Green was entitled *Making a comprehensive work: the road from bomb alley*. He used to spend his time looking out of his upstairs window with binoculars so he could spot any truants trying to leave the school. 'Bomb Alley' was an outside corridor at the school where pupils could be bullied. It was also littered with debris but – by focusing his binoculars on it as well – he managed to cut down the incidences of bullying.

He joined the Professional Association of Teachers at a time when the government was keen to give it a seat on the teachers' panel of the Burnham committee, which determined pay rises. It had inherited a situation where the NUT – because of its larger membership – was in the majority on the panel and ministers were anxious to change that situation.

His reign as general secretary of PAT certainly helped to give the association a higher profile – if only as a result of his ability to talk about the school life of various pop stars he had taught during his teaching role. One year he recalled how he had said about Francis Rossi, lead singer of Status Quo, that "he seems to think he can make a living out of playing the guitar". In giving an interview to *Globe*, an American magazine, he also revealed how he had expelled the singer Boy George from his school. "He was a perpetual truant," he said. "He wouldn't come to school and he wouldn't work when he got there ... He was weird. There was no evidence at the time that he was confused as to whether he wanted to dress up as a boy or girl. But the one thing he was not confused about – he did not want to work." (As a singer, Boy George dressed up in women's clothing and wore lipstick and make-up.) Mr Dawson's intervention stirred Boy George into writing to the *TES*, saying: "In Britain we do not encourage children to enjoy school and Eltham Green was no exception. The only real power Peter Dawson wielded was because of the existence of corporal punishment and his visual similarity to a well-known dictator." No clues as to who Boy George meant but it was widely interpreted to be a reference to Hitler.

Eventually, Mr Dawson's regime at PAT came to an end in controversy as he chose to blame single parents for all the ills of the education system in his final conference speech. In his eyes, they were responsible for low academic performance and the UK needed to turn to a greater morality to raise standards. It sparked protests from a few delegates (quite something at a PAT conference!) and prompted *The Mirror*, for whom I was then working, to run a front page article quoting the reaction of other teachers' organisations and groups representing single parents under the heading of "You're A Disgrace,

Headmaster". *The Mirror* ordered me to go and interview him the following day to see if he had changed his mind as a result of the reaction. I remember walking into the office in Derby (he had returned there from the conference) to find *The Mirror* prominently displayed on his desk. I remember frivolously thinking that I was glad they had abolished corporal punishment by then.

Anyhow, after he left, PAT (and VOICE) never quite gained the same prominence again and I believe it would be fair to say that it did not live up to the aspirations that the Conservatives had for it. One decision, taken on economic grounds, which probably did more than anything else to banish it to the ranks of the also-rans was abolishing its annual conference. It normally took place at the end of July – a quiet time in news terms – and gave it a good opportunity to promote its policies.

*****

One intriguing decision taken by Mr Carlisle in 1981 was to turn down a plan by a Conservative council to allow one of its comprehensive schools to revert back to grammar school status. The proposal would have led to the split site Erith comprehensive being replaced by a grammar and secondary modern school on separate sites. It was rejected because Mr Carlisle believed the council had not considered the impact that the proposal would have on other schools, but ironically it added to the impression that Mrs Thatcher – despite her instincts – was not exactly a friend of grammar schools. During her spell as Education Secretary in the Heath administration of 1970-4, she presided over the closure of more grammar schools than any other holder of that office. The decision, then, was symptomatic of the political stalemate between the two main political parties over the future of selection which remained for years – neither side wanting to abolish existing grammar schools or open new ones.

*****

September 1981 saw the demise of Mark Carlisle as Education Secretary and his replacement by Sir Keith Joseph – widely regarded as Mrs Thatcher's monetarist guru who was widely expected to preside over a drift to the right in education policy.

In the months before he vacated the scene in September, Mr Carlisle had trodden the path of keeping a break on government intervention in the running of schools. As described earlier, he announced he was dropping the idea of targets for the time to be devoted to core subjects in secondary schools. He also announced that there were to be no changes to the Inner London Education Authority – thus scuppering for a few years the idea put forward by the 'Sherlock' group that it should either be broken up or directly elected. This was seen in political circles as quite a coup for him and his deputy, Baroness Young.

In another decision, Mr Carlisle jettisoned a suggestion that local education authorities should publish their schools' exam results – a forerunner of league tables, if you like. Instead, he proposed that schools should publish their individual results but there was no compulsion for the local education authorities to do likewise.

His departure – though almost inevitable at some stage as he was not considered to be one of the ministers closest to Thatcher – was greeted with a tinge of sadness in education circles. "It is hard not to conceal a great deal of sympathy for Mr Mark Carlisle," said the *TES*. Relatively speaking, he had been a friend to education.

What of his successor, though? Sir Keith was moved from the Department of Industry where he had agonised over the giving out of taxpayers' money to 'lame duck' industries such as steel and shipbuilding. It was a policy that jarred with his monetarist principles – here was a complicated man full of compassion and deeply interested in the fight against poverty on the one hand but committed to support the harshest of economic policies on the other. At one time he was considered as future prime ministerial material but was characterised as 'The Mad Monk' earlier in his career after he had spoken out against the dangers of uncontrolled breeding amongst the poor.

He was probably best summed up by political adviser Stuart Sexton a couple of years after he had left office. Mr Sexton said Sir Keith spent too much time agonising over school closure decisions whilst in office, describing him as "a man who loves the debate but never the decision".

Another incident which helps complete the picture of him comes from the middle of the pay dispute with teachers when he was asked by the BBC: "Sir Keith, are teachers underpaid?" The question was followed by some 51 seconds of his silence before Sir Keith asked if they could run the question by him again.

There were, of course, fears within the profession that his monetarist zeal would lead him to make more savage cuts to education budgets than his predecessors. Amongst others there was a worry that here was a man coming to the end of his career: he no longer had hope of high office and was, according to one observer, "clearly on the way out".

His appointment to the job came just before the Conservative Party conference where he made it clear there was no more money for the sector. He also, though, told a sceptical party that they must make the best of the comprehensive system. (During the debate on education, there were cries of "shame" from the floor whenever a pro-comprehensive speaker emerged.)

He added that he was "intellectually attracted" to the idea of education vouchers – whereby parents were given money to shop around and spend the voucher at the school of their choice. Independent schools, it was argued, should also be included in the scheme. He may have been "intellectually attracted" but, in the end, he was convinced the scheme would not work as it was too bureaucratic and ended up supporting the idea of open enrolment instead. This was a practice endorsed in Kent whereby schools popular with parents were allowed to expand at the rate of one extra classroom a year to take in pupils who would otherwise have been refused a place. However, this scheme was not without its controversy. One school in Kent, the Judd school, felt it was all right to expand in the first year but that continued expansion would lead to conditions becoming overcrowded and jeopardise the standards it had achieved.

Sir Keith's comments at the Conservative Party conference – particularly over education vouchers – drew flak from former party leader Sir Edward Heath who said: "He'll split the Conservative Party from top to bottom and alienate the whole of the teaching profession."

In his first speech to a teachers' conference – the Assistant Masters and Mistresses Association – Sir Keith emphasised his economic credentials. "There is no link between the quality of education and spending policy," he said. He appeared to be getting the education world to brace itself for a time of austerity.

*****

While the education world might have been debating the significance of replacing Mark Carlisle with Sir Keith Joseph, another thorny issue was bubbling away under the surface: the future for corporal punishment in the UK.

It stemmed from a ruling by the European Court of Human Rights in late November 1980 that parents should have the right to insist that their children should not be subjected to this kind of punishment at school.

Already some education authorities – notably the Inner London Education Authority – were beginning to sense that the cane (and the tawse) had had their day and were seeking to abolish it. At this time, though, the NUT was the only teachers' organisation to support the ILEA's suggestion – most organisations believing it was a decision that should be left up to individual schools.

In July, support for abolition received powerful backing when Neil Kinnock, then Labour's education spokesman, pledged a future Labour government would abolish the cane and promised there would be a three-line whip (no pun intended!) to drive the measure through Parliament.

At this stage, though, there was little enthusiasm in government circles to be seen as coming out in support of abolishing corporal punishment – even though the UK was soon to be left as the only country in Europe still to sanction its use. The last 30 years or so might have ushered in a trend of politicians taking more control of what went on in schools, but this was an example of the opposite: ministers did not under any circumstances want to be seen as encouraging its demise in case they were seen as being weak on discipline.

*****

As an aside, the perils of allowing a journalist to go on a school trip were emphasized when my colleague, Stephen Cohen, went on board the cruise ship SS Uganda which was taking schoolchildren on a tour of the Greek islands, Turkey, Sicily and Egypt. On board with him were 14 officials from Berkshire County Council, the chairman of the education committee and some of their wives – taking advantage of 'freebie' places. They did help supervise the children during the day but sat at the captain's table and attended a sequence of cocktail parties during the evenings. Peter Edwards, director of education, said the party was there to find out if parents were getting value for money. The resulting furore, though, was followed by the chairman of the education committee resigning before the local elections in May. *

*****

Sir Keith Joseph began the New Year, 1982, by spelling out more of his philosophy on education. He used his speech to the North of England Education Conference – traditionally at that time used by the Secretary of State to set out his or her stall for the next 12 months – to call for the removal of ineffective

---

*   This was to have been one of SS Uganda's last school trips. The following year – halfway through a cruise for children – it was recquisitioned by the government to act as a hospital ship for wounded service personnel during the Falklands War.

teachers by compulsory redundancies. Getting rid of so-called incompetent teachers has always been a vexed issue with many a Secretary of State or their deputy seeking to score political points by taking steps to make it easier for schools or local education authorities to do so. Sir Keith was treading a path which, in time, would be trodden by Labour's Schools Minister Stephen Byers after the 1997 election and, on taking up his job as Chief Inspector of Schools, Chris Woodhead. As to Sir Keith's intervention, it came at a turbulent time in relationships between the teachers' unions, local education authorities and the government as the profession headed towards industrial action over the 1982 pay claim.

For good measure, Sir Keith also announced he was now "intellectually attracted" to the idea of student loans – a plan which had been on the backburner in government circles for several months but was facing massive opposition from student unions. It now looked as if it was facing a revival in government circles.

Later in the year, he fleshed out more details of the scheme, saying that he hoped the package for students would offer them 50 per cent grants and 50 per cent loans.

In an interview, he also said it had been "wicked" to remove grammar schools (although, in keeping with his speech to his party conference the previous year, he did not outline any plan to bring them back). He said that he would be concentrating on ensuring the education system was relevant to the bottom 40 per cent, saying he was "personally disturbed about the 40 per cent for whom examinations are not a passport".

He later unveiled plans to give local authorities grants for schemes aimed at helping that bottom 40 per cent – but a £2 million ceiling on the package led to criticism that it was too 'small beer' a scheme to achieve much. Sir Keith indicated that the types of schemes he would like to see would be more work experience for pupils and greater co-operation between schools and colleges in providing a curriculum tailor-made for the bottom 40 per cent.

On vouchers, the other idea to which he was "intellectually attracted", he told the Conservative Party conference of his support for the idea. "At present the choice of going to an independent school is open to those who are well-off and, now that we have an Assisted Places Scheme, to some of those who are clever," he said. "But the Conservative Party is not concerned only with the rich and clever. We want to extend choice to every person." As to implementation, though, he watered down his aspirations and cited the Kent open enrolment scheme as a sign of the kind of policy he "would like to see more of".

All in all, his comments seemed to denote a shift rightwards from the era of Mark Carlisle. What remained to be seen, though, was whether he had the ability to deliver on the agenda he was setting himself.

In the meantime, the NUT appeared to be shifting leftwards, causing me to proclaim on its last day at conference that year that I had witnessed "20 of the most radical minutes in the history of NUT conferences". During that time, it had passed a motion declaring that teachers should not have to cover for absent colleagues and it also voted in favour of campaigning to abolish the cane. For good measure, the previous day, it had voted to campaign in favour of unilateral disarmament – although it stopped short of deciding to affiliate to the Campaign for Nuclear Disarmament. It was a radical shift in the union's position – previously such a move was considered "outside the aims and objectives of the union" on the grounds it was not concerned with education issues or teachers' pay and working conditions. It got round that by suggesting a nuclear holocaust would affect teachers – not necessarily a frivolous point.

Of the three moves, the decision to campaign for the abolition of the cane was probably the most significant one. The UK was in a cleft stick in the wake of the decision by the European Court of Human Rights that parents had the right to insist that their children should not be subjected to corporal punishment. Logically, it meant that heads must find out from every parent whether they would consent to their children being caned. It also threw up the prospect of two children being found guilty of the same offence – one of whom could be caned while the other who would have to be spared the rod. Small wonder, then, that the Secondary Heads Association – the precursor of the Association of School and College Leaders – was given advice from its legal adviser, Roland Browne, that heads would ignore parental wishes at their peril and risk becoming a test case in an English court if they caned a pupil in defiance of a parent's wishes. Later during the conference season, the mood of members at the National Association of Head Teachers signified that they felt it was inevitable that corporal punishment would have to be abolished. However, speaking at the PAT conference, which he chose to attend rather than the NUT, Sir Keith said there was no prospect of early legislation on corporal punishment.

The matter, of course, was likely to be taken out of his hands. A dozen cases had now been lodged with the European Court of Human Rights asking it to rule that corporal punishment was a "degrading" punishment. If the court so ruled, the government did not have a decision to make.

*****

It is perhaps worth noting at this stage that a glance through the August editions of the newspapers reveals very little interest in O-level and A-level results. The results were not published by the exam boards and there seemed to be little enthusiasm in newspapers for stories about them. The only mention of A-levels in the *TES* this year, for instance, was a paragraph saying that Prince Edward had passed A-levels in English literature, history and economics. Even then, it did not say what grades he had achieved.

Reporting of exam results only began in earnest after the GCSE replaced O-levels in 1988 – possibly on the grounds that the percentage of the cohort taking the exam was now much higher and there was therefore more public interest in them. The exam boards also got together to form an umbrella organisation which published national results for the first time. Also, as universities increased their student intake, so the numbers taking A-levels increased again, creating more parental interest in the results.

Nowadays, of course, you cannot move for speculation about the results in advance of their publication and analysis of what they mean after publication.

Figures show that the percentage of pupils obtaining A to C grade passes at GCSE in its second year of operation had risen from 42.5 per cent to 46.1 per cent. In later years such a rise would be accompanied by claims of grade inflation and protests that the exams were getting easier. Possibly a more likely explanation at this stage was that teachers had become more used to teaching the syllabus. Also, I remember reading research which showed the entire increase was down to the improvements in the performance of girls. If the exams had been "dumbed down", it argued, it would mean we had some very thick boys in the education system compared to yesteryear.

What is certain, though, is that the exam season is more stressful for students now than it was when I took my A-levels. Back then, a card arrived from the school the following day to inform me of my grades. Had I taken them today, I would have been down at the school gates at 9am on the day of publication – or even earlier – clamouring to find out the results.

*****

Towards the end of the year, Sir Keith Joseph announced he had decided that HMI reports on individual schools should be published from the beginning of January. At the time that he spoke, there were around 200 reports in the pipeline.

Interestingly, this announcement failed to ignite much controversy – probably because the HMI reports were not as controversial as today's reports by Ofsted, the education standards watchdog. There was no ranking of schools as 'outstanding', 'good', 'requires improvement' or 'inadequate' as there is today. The head's job did not appear to be on the line as it is today if governors sniff that he or she is not performing as well as they ought do.

Nevertheless, this was an important step along the path to making schools more accountable, which helped shape events to come.

*****

Interestingly, David Hart, the general secretary of the NAHT, this year became the first teachers' leader to point his finger at "blatant acts of political interference in the running of schools". He chose it as the theme of his conference speech and cited a case in Lancashire where governors were urged "to choose a chairman who is able to stand up to the headteacher". "Governors should learn to read between the lines of the headteacher's report because it is as important for what it conceals as to what it reveals," the speech went on. A sign of things to come.

TIMELINE

1980

Clegg Commission recommends pay rise of between 17 per cent and 25 per cent for teachers.

Government rejects the first application from a Conservative council to allow a comprehensive school to revert to grammar school status.

Independent schools publish A-level results for the first time (collectively not individually).

1981

Government backs down on the introduction of a framework for the curriculum – specifying the times that should be spent on core subjects. It also backs down on compelling local education authorities to publish the exam results of individual schools – thus removing the possibility that local league tables could be compiled.

Sir Keith Joseph replaces Mark Carlisle as Education Secretary.

1982

Government announces grants to help teach the bottom 40 per cent.

Headteachers say they will have to bow to the inevitable and see corporal punishment banned.

Plans for 50 per cent grants, 50 per cent loans for undergraduates unveiled.

HMI reports on individual schools to be published, declares Sir Keith Joseph.

Chapter Two
Trouble and Strife

The 1983 New Year dawned with the political parties putting their finishing touches on their parties' General Election manifestos. At first it seemed as if the Conservatives would go forward with a radical manifesto including the two ideas to which Sir Keith Joseph had become "intellectually attracted": vouchers for parents so they could chose their children's schools; and student loans.

The cabinet is said on the first count to have told Sir Keith early in February that members wanted to see a more radical scheme than the one on offer. In particular, they wanted to see poorly performing schools – defined for this purpose as those put down by few parents as their children's first choice school – penalised. In the worst case scenario, those with too few pupils would have to close, thus allowing market forces to dictate the future of the education system.

In March, ministers also drafted their student loans scheme which – as expected – recommended replacing half the student grant with a loan.

However, by the time the election manifesto was published, both ideas had been dropped in favour of a more conservative (with a small c) approach to education – thus denting the theory that the Thatcher government always adopted a radical right approach to policy making

As an alternative policy, Sir Keith floated the idea of separate technical schools for pupils to enhance vocational skills. Within a month, about one in three local councils had put in bids to run these type of schools but a significant number of Labour-controlled metropolitan authorities boycotted the scheme on the grounds it was yet another attempt to divide pupils into "sheep and goats" and that the technical schools would, in effect, become something akin to secondary modern schools at the end of the day.

In promoting this agenda, Sir Keith talked of "separate but equal strands of schooling for pupils" but pointed out that an attempt to introduce technical schools as part of the 1944 Education Act had, in the main, been a failure. Somewhat ruefully, he added: "The holder of my office has no power to say what is going on in the classroom and quite right, too." It was almost as if he was prophesying the failure of the scheme that he had just announced. In the event, the idea did re-emerge in the shape of the privately sponsored City Technology Colleges promoted by his successor, Kenneth Baker.

Sir Keith's comments about the extent (or limit) of his powers were challenged later on in the year by Sir James Hamilton, a former Permanent Secretary at the Department of Education and Science, who said he felt the department should have more control of what was taught in schools. The government had shown too much "delicacy" about making its presence felt in the classroom. "I believe we erred on the side of safety," he went on.

This argument, though, was for the future. On the ground in 1983, Labour, too, was running into trouble with its manifesto. The party was still committed to end private schooling through a ruthless weeding out of independent schools' charitable status. However, it emerged in March that a hitherto unpublished document from the European Court of Human Rights ruled that removing a school's charitable status was just as big a violation of human rights as an outright ban on allowing private education. Independent schools themselves also entered the fray by launching a "stop Labour" campaign, aimed at preserving their charitable status with emphasis on the scholarships they provided for pupils from poorer homes and those they took in under the government's Assisted Places Scheme.

The other main strand of Labour's election manifesto was a pledge to restore the cuts in education with the injection of £1.76 billion a year into the education budget. Despite this, a poll of 550 teachers on the eve of the election by the *TES* revealed that 44 per cent would be voting Conservative, 28 per cent for the Liberal/Social Democrat Alliance and only 26 per cent would be voting for Labour. Significantly, the poll did not go into what had shaped their voting intentions so it could well have been policies other than education. It did lead to some in the camp of Neil Kinnock, still Labour's education spokesman, describing the teachers as "turkeys voting for Christmas". Mrs Thatcher's poll ratings had been boosted since reclaiming the Falkland Islands from Argentina – whilst Labour's election manifesto was described as "the longest suicide note in history" with its emphasis on more nationalisation and nuclear disarmament.

In any event, the Conservatives won the election with a comfortable majority – and it was business as usual in the aftermath, with Sir Keith being returned as Education Secretary as Mrs Thatcher drew up her cabinet. A week after the election, Mrs Thatcher put the final nail in the coffin of the voucher scheme by saying she had backed off the idea because she considered it to be unworkable. She, too, threw her weight behind the open enrolment scheme being practised in Kent – which was to emerge as policy set in stone in her third term of office when she finally got around to some serious reform of the education system with the GERBIL. However, the initial portents for the scheme were not that good. In the Medway Towns, the most popular school, Chatham South, appealed against being ordered to expand because of its popularity. It said its site was not big enough to cope with the expansion from 600 to 700 pupils that the open enrolment scheme dictated. It won its appeal, thereby throwing a question mark over how extensive were the powers of the local authority to carry out the reform.

*****

By far the most momentous event of Mrs Thatcher's second term in office was the continuous battle between the government and the teachers' unions over pay.

Indeed, the telltale signs that industrial strife was in the wind emerged before the election when salary negotiations looked as though they were heading for stalemate.

Leaders of the local authorities – specifically the Conservative-controlled Association of County Councils – were determined to clip the wings of the teachers' unions. To their mind, the teachers could too easily resort to a ban on voluntary duties – including the key one of midday supervision – which could effectively cause chaos in schools, forcing secondary heads to send pupils out of school because they did not have enough staff left to supervise them. In addition, some primary schools had been forced to close at lunchtime as a result of this sanction.

The ACC started off in determined mood, saying there would be no pay rise unless progress was made in talks on teachers' conditions of service aimed at drawing up a new contract which would clarify the issue of lunchtime supervision. One suggestion was that teachers should be paid for it – thus imposing a financial penalty on them if they withdrew from voluntary activities.

In the event, the real crunch was put off until the following year when the local authorities offered teachers – who had been seeking an unspecified 'substantial rise' – just a three per cent pay increase. The teachers' unions rejected the offer with both the NUT and NASUWT warning there could well be a long drawn-out dispute. The NASUWT immediately put forward plans for a half-day strike while the NUT opted for a one-day strike in May. Both unions also said they were under pressure from their members to take action that would disrupt that summer's examinations. The threat of militancy had the effect of causing a split in the employers' side in negotiations with Mike Bower, the Labour chairman of Sheffield City Council, calling for the dispute to go to arbitration. Labour eventually requisitioned another meeting of the Burnham committee in an attempt to avoid industrial action by following this route. It was held against a background of militancy with Doug McAvoy, deputy general secretary of the NUT (and leader of the teachers' side in negotiations due to an injury suffered by Fred Jarvis), warning that there was "every prospect of extended strike action" following the one-day stoppage in May.

In the event, the employers did raise their offer to 4.5 per cent – described as "too little, too late" by Mr McAvoy. As the leader of the teachers' side in the negotiations, McAvoy, a former PE teacher and a tough-talking Geordie, presented a no-nonsense approach to the pay talks. Within weeks of the negotiations failing, all three unions had opted for a ban on all voluntary activities – lunchtime supervision and covering for absent colleagues being the most effective weapons – leading to schools closing, school meals staff being sent home and attempts by some authorities to dock teachers' pay. In Humberside, for instance, the county council decided to dock the pay of those who refused to cover lessons for absent colleagues. The NUT was pondering a further escalation of the dispute with the prospect of an all-out strike in the autumn term but there was just a glimmer of hope that the employers' side might be prepared to go to arbitration. At this point, though, they were sticking to a demand that the teachers should reduce their demand for a 12.5 per cent rise – the figure they had ultimately put on their call for a 'substantial' rise.

Eventually, the teachers relented and the pay dispute went to arbitration in late June with Doreen Jones, president of the moderate Assistant Masters and Mistresses Association, warning that the decision was likely to be just a temporary truce in a longer running battle. Teachers went back to resuming so-called "voluntary duties" but – in reality – many individual teachers decided not to resume things like lunchtime supervision and out-of-hours activities like school sporting events. One headteacher summed up the morale in schools by saying they were "a dreadful place to be". "We did not finish our rugby, soccer, netball or hockey fixtures," he added. "We have not even started our tennis or cricket. Our athletics track is silent and no one is running. We do not do Duke of Edinburgh Awards week. Our charity efforts have ceased. Sixty clubs meeting once weekly have been discontinued. Yet nobody is on strike."

If anything, the arbitration award – made in September – backed up Doreen Jones's warning. It awarded the teachers 5.1 per cent (only a little more than had originally been on the table) but did nothing to tackle the long-running sore over voluntary activities. One of the awards panel, Professor John Hughes, dissented from the final offer, saying it would have a dangerous effect on the morale in schools and that teachers should have been considered a case for a special rise. Professor Eric Armstrong, chairman of the arbitration panel, suggested that arbitration in future would not be the best way to settle the teachers' pay claim – a comment that a now revitalised Fred Jarvis agreed with. Professor Armstrong said there should be a teachers' pay review body – a request that Kenneth Baker subsequently acceded to. Even Sir Philip Merridale, the Conservative councillor from Hampshire who led the management side in negotiations, said: "I can imagine that teachers who were misled into expecting that independent arbitrators would recommend a higher settlement may be disappointed." The NUT's reaction to the award was that it would be planning to campaign for a 12 per cent settlement in 1985.

The fragile peace inevitably shattered in the New Year when Sir Keith Joseph said he could see no prospect of financing an extra rise on top of the pay award for teachers to cover a new teachers' contract. Strike action was resumed by the teachers in February as the authorities offered just four per cent. I can remember at this juncture being invited to go on the Jimmy Young show on Radio 2 to talk about the effect of the teachers' strikes – something which was to forge a lasting bond between my future in-laws and me. I felt flummoxed when Jimmy Young introduced me by saying: "And now we have Richard Garner of the *Times Educational Supplement* on the prog who's going to tell us how many schools are shut today because of the teachers' strike." Oh, ****, I thought! My mind went blank but I remembered an NUT press release which said it was calling out teachers in 215 schools so I crossed my fingers and mumbled "About 200, Jimmy." It obviously didn't come across quite as badly as I feared, though, because when my new partner, Anne – later my wife – introduced me for the first time to her parents that weekend, her mother said: "Oh, you're the one who was on the Jimmy Young show this week." Made it! Five years of reporting for the *TES*, no recognition. Three minutes on the Jimmy Young show and an instant celebrity! I have got something to be thankful to the *TES* for, though. I suspect that one of the reasons why Anne, a college lecturer, agreed to go out with me was that I could get her the *TES* on a Thursday evening instead of her having to wait for Friday morning so she could get a head start in pursuing all the job adverts. Actually, the relationship went deeper than that. Fed up with cuts and reorganisations, she finally left education and retrained as a chiropodist – something I definitely could not help her with.

I digress, though. The dispute continued and Sir Philip Merridale, who believed he would be ousted as his council's representative on the management panel, gave an uncharacteristically frank interview on the negotiations, and accused Sir Keith Joseph of "persistent stubbornness" on teachers' pay. "As I ride off into the sunset, I want to leave you with a final message – and that is the government's persistent stubbornness will sow the seeds of its undoing," he said. Trouble was, he survived and didn't ride off into the sunset – and had to try and present a united management front with Sir Keith again!

Sir Keith, who was having a rough ride for his handling of the dispute, suffered further embarrassment when Keith Brown, spokesman for the Conservative Trade Unionists' group, resigned as a comprehensive school teacher after writing in protest to Sir Keith about the lack of pay and promotion prospects in the profession.

Meanwhile, the teachers had their own enemies – incurring the wrath of former Beatle Paul McCartney, who sent his children to state schools and tore up their leaflets as he took his children to school. He was annoyed at the disruption it was causing to his children.

The only thaw in the dispute came about as Sir Keith announced his review of the teachers' panel of the Burnham committee, leading to the NUT losing its overall majority for the first time. Returns to the review gave the NUT a membership of 210,000 compared to a total of 224,812 for all the other unions combined. As a result, the NUT was given 13 members in the new panel compared to a combined 15 members for the other unions who agreed to resume negotiations now the NUT was no longer in the driving seat. Finally, the other unions agreed a 6.9 per cent deal – rising to 8.5 per cent by the end of March, leaving the NUT in isolated opposition to it. The deal was finally sealed in March 1986 just as the new pay negotiating round began.

After days in negotiations on the new pay round, a fresh deal covering the new contract for teachers was agreed between the two sides costing 16.4 per cent on the pay bill. However, it proved not to be acceptable to Kenneth Baker, who had by now succeeded Sir Keith as Education Secretary (of which more anon). He proposed his own package – costing, according to DES sources, £85 million less and with less emphasis on the lower paid ranks of teachers but a better deal for senior management. It was the sort of deal that Sir Keith, with his monetarist principles, would have shirked from. Kenneth Baker, though, was determined to sort out the dispute. The package was to be phased in over 18 months and, crucially, included winding up the Burnham pay negotiating machinery. (Some people might argue that it is a misnomer to call it pay negotiating machinery as, on most occasions, both sides had failed to agree, with claims going to arbitration.) There was no word at this stage as to what would replace Burnham – but a front-runner appeared to be a pay review body which ministers believed would take the sting out of salary disputes and reduce the chances of industrial action in the classroom. In the meantime, an interim advisory committee on pay was being set up to cover the next two years. The government finally imposed its deal in March 1987 – just two months before the next General Election. It took out a two-page ad in the *TES* to promote the package. Mr Baker claimed "I have won a large victory", referring to the extra 18.8 per cent for the education budget as a result of the deal. The strikes continued, though – this time in opposition to the loss of negotiating rights through the scrapping of the Burnham committee. However, the signs were that the industrial action was on its last legs. A MORI poll said only one in three parents believed teachers were underpaid and 54 per cent thought they are wrong to strike over the decision to remove their negotiating rights. Gradually, opposition to the Baker deal was whittled down, leaving the NASUWT isolated in opposing it. In April 1988, after four years of strife, the teacher union conference season witnessed a rare wave of moderation, with all three unions saying there was unlikely to be industrial action over the interim advisory committee's first report, which by then had been published and recommended a 4.25 per cent pay deal.

So, after a grim four years at the chalkface, peace was finally restored to the classroom. It took two significant events to achieve: the review of the Burnham committee, whittling away the NUT's inbuilt majority on the teachers' side of the panel – thus allowing for a thaw in negotiations at a crucial time during the dispute – plus Kenneth Baker's donning of the mantle of Education Secretary. Teachers' unions may not have liked his uncompromising approach in imposing the pay deal but at least he had secured more money from the Treasury to finance the deal, unlike his predecessor. Also, even if they did not like his setting up of the interim advisory committee and, subsequently, pay review body, at least for the most part it brought a touch of independence to the procedure for settling teachers' pay. Also, I have heard a few teachers' leaders arguing that at least they made some progress in their pay dispute compared with other industrial groups at that time – notably the miners. The new contract, too, freed them from any moral obligation to take part in lunchtime supervision duties.

Just as a footnote to this period of teacher militancy, consider this: AMMA, the most moderate of the three big teachers' unions who did not join in most of the industrial action, did in fact vote for indefinite strike action at one school – West Derby Church of England primary school in Liverpool – where its three members voted unanimously in favour of action over the caretaker using their staff room to brew up of a morning. The GMB, the caretakers' union, would not talk to AMMA as it was not a member of the TUC. However, by law, the teachers were in the right because legislation states they should be able to have their own staff room in schools! Odd what kind of issues can become a matter of principle!

*****

Talking about militancy brings me on to another dispute affecting the education sector in the 1980s: the stance adopted by the militant-dominated Liverpool City Council over rate-capping.

In February 1984, Liverpool warned its staff to start saving as the city was likely to go broke. The Labour-led authority was planning to set an illegal budget by implementing a 'no job losses, no cuts' policy whilst at the same time opting for no excessive rate increases – which would have been necessary to finance the first pledge.

It was, of course, the conflict that was singled out by Neil Kinnock in his Labour Party conference speech when he rounded on the spectacle of a Labour council "sending out redundancy notices by taxi".

In truth, it was stranger than that. The controversy continued until September 1985 when Liverpool headteachers indicated they might work for no pay if the city really did run out of money. The city council told staff that they would not be paid beyond the end of the month.

At the same time, as council workers staged a one-day strike over the situation, Liverpool's Director of Education Kenneth Antcliffe had to work from a cellar bar round the corner from his office as he could not get into the council buildings which had been locked by caretaking staff.

The headteachers were then warned they could be disciplined and surcharged if they failed to deliver redundancy notices to their teaching staff. That plan was scuppered at some schools when the teaching staff walked out and the headteachers refused to cross their picket lines and were thus unable to gain access to the redundancy notices. The taxis that had been hired to deliver the redundancy notices – as a result – could find no one to deliver them to and so flung them through open windows in the hope that they would be picked up by someone some time. The redundancy notices said they would be laid off from January 1 and re-employed in April when the new budget came into effect.

In the event, the council workers action escalated and as many as 300 council staff had to resort to working in a city centre pub. Mr Antcliffe somehow negotiated a deal whereby he could gain access to his office through a subterranean passageway. The long-running dispute was eventually ended when 47 Labour councillors were disqualified from holding office and the Liberal/Social Democrat Alliance took over the running of the city. There was one bit of joy for the teachers from all this, though. In a final parting act before they left office, the Labour councillors signed the first ever agreement in the history of education giving guaranteed preparation and marking time for teachers – a deal which the Alliance promised to honour.

*****

And so, back to corporal punishment: finally, in November 1984, the government reacted to the European court ruling that parents should have the right to insist their children were not beaten at school. It published legislation giving parents the right to exempt their children from such punishment – but which allowed schools to retain the sanction.

By now, though, the debate had moved on and most people in the education world believed the only sane way to treat this situation was by abolishing the cane altogether. Sir Keith Joseph, introducing the legislation, said schools would have to ask parents whether they would be prepared to allow the school to beat their children. However, an unlikely alliance of the NUT, PAT and Society of Teachers Opposed to Physical Punishment, an anti-corporal punishment pressure group, opposed the Bill, with Peter Dawson, general secretary of PAT, wryly remarking: "It takes an extraordinary government decision to unite us but they have done it. It is unthinkable to have two disciplinary codes operating in the same school."

The legislation looked set for a rough passage through Parliament. Already there were Conservatives who believed abolition was the right answer – such as Robert Key, the Conservative MP for Salisbury. Giles Radice, by then Labour's shadow education spokesman, accused Sir Keith of "ducking the issue". As the MPs debated the Bill, a growing number of authorities passed motions outlawing the use of corporal punishment in their schools. There were seven Conservative rebels when the Bill came to its second reading. One of them,

Tony Marlow, MP for Northampton North and not a noted moderate, said it was obvious that if a child wanted to commit a misdemeanour he should do it with a fellow pupil whose parents forbad him to be caned so that he could escape the punishment. However, despite the rebellion, the Bill sailed through the Commons unaltered. However, it met with more opposition in the Lords where a motion which would have led to its abolition was passed by 108 votes to 104. One of those who voted for abolition, Lord Onslow, said: "I think we have all wanted to thrash our children and I quite understand the schoolteachers who want to thrash the children in their class. However, to be able to thrash Johnny but not Fred would be ridiculous and unfair." It was not just the forces of enlightenment, then, that were opposed to the Bill. As the debate continued Berkshire became the first Conservative-controlled authority to vote for abolition. In a sign of the times, too, Tom Scott, the former teacher who ran STOPP – a dedicated campaigner – decided to quit his job to launch into a new career in the theatre: "The question is now no longer 'will corporal punishment be banned?' but 'when?'," he said as he announced his decision. It was not until after the 1987 election, though, that the punishment entered its final death throes in the UK. In July 1987, it was announced MPs would have a free vote on the issue. The decision to abolish corporal punishment was finally taken on July 22 that year. It squeaked through narrowly by one vote with Mrs Thatcher unable to attend because she had to attend an official dinner for Nancy Reagan. About a dozen other MPs were caught up in traffic outside the Commons as a practice for the Royal Wedding of Prince Charles and Princess Diana and failed to attend. In all, 35 Conservatives voted in favour of abolition. Ministers were said to have been privately relieved the vote went the way it did – it went through without them having been seen to support the idea of abolition.

When I look back at my 36 years covering education, I think this must have been one of the most significant decisions that was taken during that time. It doesn't say a great deal for us that we were the last country in Europe to stop beating children in our schools – indeed, four years after the rest of the continent had banned it. We always have been out of step with them! At least we managed to do it in the end.

*****

There were other important decisions taken during the lifetime of this Parliament. In June 1984, Sir Keith Joseph finally put his seal of approval to the plan to replace O-levels and CSEs with one exam – to be called the General Certificate of Secondary Education. Courses would start in September,

1986, with the first exams being sat in the summer of 1988. The decision was described by one source as "putting the sheep and goats back together again".

Sir Keith had come under tremendous pressure from within the Conservative Party to back down on this proposal – first mooted during Shirley Williams's tenure as Education Secretary in the last years of the Callaghan administration. However, the Conservative-controlled Association of County Councils favoured the reform. Fred Jarvis, of the NUT, said: "This is one decision of his which will be applauded throughout the teaching profession. Our own union proposed such a move 15 years ago."

Indeed, the exam boards had been working on the national criteria for the new exam for some time while they awaited Sir Keith's final go-ahead. Under the new arrangements, an A to C grade was considered worthy of an O-level and the exam boards who offered O-levels were put in charge of developing the criteria for these grades.

The introduction of the GCSE – taken by the vast majority of the 600,000 a year age cohort at 16 – sparked off far more interest in exams than there had ever been before. It brought to an end the period where there had been very little coverage of exam results – the boards began publishing details of the results and the numbers taking each subject once the GCSE was up and running. Of course, now you cannot move from wall-to-wall coverage of results day with plenty of advance speculation as to what the results will be.

The future make-up of the Inner London Education Authority also became clearer at this time as it emerged there would be direct elections to the authority from 1986, with an interim board of borough nominees controlling the authority between the demise of the GLC and the introduction of the new system.

Of course, the directly elected ILEA did not last long. By 1988, with the new authority only just into its first term of directly elected councillors, the government was seeking its abolition. Under the government plan, local councils would take responsibility for running education from 1990. In a statement justifying the decision, Mr Baker said: "Its [the ILEA's] spending is profligate, its service is poor. Between 1981 and 1988 its spending increased from £700 million to more than £1 billion. The increase in expenditure has in no way been reflected in improved pupil performance which remains disappointingly low." Inner London boroughs warned that they would face financial and staffing crises if they were to take over the running of the service. However, Mr Baker promised that teachers would keep their jobs.

It would be fair to say there was a great deal of concern, particularly in

Labour circles, over the measures. However, several of the London boroughs have made terrific strides in the past two decades towards improving the performance of their pupils. The London Challenge, introduced by Labour, saw London improve its exam results to such an extent that they became the best in the country. Researchers have come up with many reasons why this may have occurred, including the introduction of Teach First, which saw the most talented graduates (who hadn't studied education at university) move into London schools; while another report claimed that the rise in exam passes was down to demographic trends which saw the number of Asian pupils, renowned for their hard work ethic, increase in London's schools. One of the achievements that has most stuck in my mind, though, is how Tower Hamlets, where the majority of pupils have English as a second language, outscored Kent – often dubbed "the garden of England" – in National Curriculum tests for 11-year-olds in reading.

There was another blow to the hopes of those Conservatives campaigning for a return to grammar schools at about this time as Solilhull in the West Midlands at first proposed to return two of its secondary comprehensive schools to grammar school status and then, after scenting opposition, refined this to a more modest proposal for one. It finally abandoned the idea after a poll of parents showed immense opposition to it. In all, more than 90 per cent of those who voted registered their opposition to it. A philosophical Michael Ellis, chairman of Solihull's education committee, said: "There's no point in consulting if you pay no attention to what parents said."

Meanwhile, the unpopularity of the Thatcher administration in the education world grew. It probably reached its zenith when Oxford dons voted in February 1985 to withhold an honorary doctorate from the Prime Minister by 738 votes to 319 in protest at the effect her policies were having on education "from the provision for the nursery child to the most advanced research". The decision brought an orgy of recrimination upon their heads from the media. *The Express*, for instance, said: "Their decision is ungracious, petulant and adolescent"; the *Mail* called it "a vindictive demo by narrow-minded academics" and "spiteful";. while *The Times* said the decision was "in no way worthy of respect – it is the culmination of a nasty campaign which has oscillated between political spite and logic chopping". Sadly, *The Guardian* did not have a leader that day.

A more concrete sign of the shift in popularity came with the usual eve-of-polling poll of teachers' voting intentions in 1987. It showed 46 per cent intended to vote for the Liberal/Social Democratic Party Alliance, 28 per cent for Labour and 24 per cent for the Conservatives. As Neil Kinnock might have put it: "The turkeys have stopped voting for Christmas."

TIMELINE

1983

HMI reports on individual schools published for the first time.

Vouchers for parents to choose schools and student loans dropped.

1984

New Year starts with Bernard Crick, George Orwell's biographer, saying *1984* should not be taught in schools as it was too complex to be handled at O-level.

Solihull parents reject a return to grammar schools.

Teachers' pay strikes begin.

Government decides ILEA should be directly elected.

Sir Keith gives the go-ahead for the GCSE to replace O-levels and CSEs, first exams to be sat in 1988.

1985

Oxford academics withhold honorary degree from Mrs Thatcher.

Government White Paper calls for legislation to ensure teachers receive an annual appraisal.

NUT loses its overall majority on teachers' panel of the Burnham committee, opening up the prospect of further talks on pay.

1986

Sir Keith Joseph is greeted with complete silence as he addresses the NASUWT conference.

Kenneth Baker replaces Sir Keith as Education Secretary.

Decision to outlaw corporal punishment is finally taken in the Commons.

Government announces it will impose 16.4 per cent pay deal spread over 18 months – coupled with new teachers' contract.

Fresh strike action over plan to dismantle Burnham committee, thus taking away teachers' negotiating rights.

Chapter Three
The Day of the GERBIL

In reality, the launching pad for Mrs Thatcher's education reforms of the late 1980s was just after the local government elections in 1986. The Conservatives had done very badly, with blame for the teacher dispute and disruption to children's education probably resting on their shoulders in many people's eyes. Labour won outright control of seven authorities in London and the Metropolitan districts. The Conservatives lost overall control in a further seven.

Interviewed about the results, Mrs Thatcher made the comment: "We must do something about education." Understated words.

Something was done within a couple of weeks of the polls. Sir Keith Joseph, who had already announced his decision to retire as an MP at the next election, was replaced by Kenneth Baker.

During his spell at the DES, Sir Keith gave the impression of a man who was deeply tortured about the decisions he had to make. Privately, he cared very deeply about injustice but his intellect prevented him from making humane decisions based on cases of disadvantage that he came across. Those private virtues were sometimes a public liability – hence his prevarication when asked by an interviewer at the height of the teachers' dispute as to whether teachers were underpaid. He also agonised for months over the decision as to whether to replace O-levels and CSEs with a new 16-plus exam, the GCSE. In the end, in a decision that some might have considered to be contrary to his natural instincts, he gave it the go-ahead.

He left his office with education – if not in a state of crisis – deeply troubled by the long-running teachers' dispute. His own instinct was not to seek extra public spending to get the government out of a hole. As a result, he alienated both the teachers' unions and the local authority management – at that stage controlled by the Conservatives. He failed to show any flexibility or much leadership during the dispute which, inevitably, took up much of the spotlight during the years that he was at the helm. As a result, he will probably be remembered more for what he did not achieve during his years at the helm than what he did. He had also failed to act decisively over corporal punishment with the result that government legislation – which favoured merely giving parents the right to exempt their children from being caned – was meandering slowly through the House of Parliament. It was ultimately defeated after he left office. However, his decision to bring in the GCSE can count as a significant reform to the exam system.

Kenneth Baker, on the other hand, was much more of a pragmatist. He would not be hidebound by any "intellectual conviction" that would hamper him from asking for more public resources for education. Indeed, he would fight tooth and nail in cabinet for extra resources and eventually put forward a 16.4 per cent package – linked to a new teachers' contract – which in the end was enough to bring to an end successive years of industrial action in schools. Okay, he still had to impose it on the teachers' unions and, controversially in their eyes, linked it to taking away their negotiating rights and replacing them ultimately with a pay review body. However, there was a feeling in the end that the teachers should quit while they were ahead and concentrate on what they had achieved rather than continue fighting for what they had not.

Mr Baker's first major education reform was to unveil plans for a network of City Technical Colleges. There were to be 20 of them funded by the government and business with the first of them opening in 1988. They would contain in their curriculum a "strong practical element" considered necessary to prepare pupils for the world of employment. They would, he told the Conservative Party conference to rapturous cheers, be free from local education authority control and may introduce a longer school day so that they could fit in a broad and balanced curriculum alongside practical skills. He was anxious – as he has been in more recent years, such as when he was behind the initiative to set up a network of University Technical Colleges throughout the country – that he should not just attract 'sheep' but 'goats' as well to become pupils in these schools.

While Mr Baker put forward modest proposals for 20 new CTCs, the Conservative right was quick to seize on the initiative with Bob Dunn, a junior minister considered to be its authentic voice within the DES, arguing that the number could be expanded to 220 or possibly 420 in the future.

Mr Baker's next initiative, announced in a television interview, comprised plans to legislate the curriculum. The announcement appeared to catch his officials on the hop as DES sources expressed some surprise at his comments. Mr Baker, though, put flesh on the bones of his comments saying he wanted "more benchmarks, more central control of the curriculum", although he stressed that what he did not want was a "completely regimented" system. He floated the idea of setting attainment targets for 7, 11 and 14-year-olds – thus paving the way for the SATs tests which have caused so much controversy in the ensuing years. Interestingly enough, it was stressed at the beginning that the level four target set for the test for 11-year-olds should not be seen as a pass/fail mark. It was set at the level that an average child should reach. Therefore, those politicians who have decried the fact that only 50 per cent reached the attainment target at the outset were missing the point – sometimes wilfully, I would say, in an attempt to discredit opponents of the reforms. One unnamed minister is said to have asked bemused officials at one point: "Why are there 50 per cent of kids who are below the average?" He was obviously not a candidate for a level four rating in maths himself.

The plans for the new assessment regime were quickly followed by a broader outline of what the National Curriculum should contain. All pupils should receive a grounding in maths, English, science, a foreign language (from the age of 11), history, geography and technology. The tests for 7, 11 and 14-year-olds should be set and marked by the teachers themselves but moderated externally. It was only after a boycott of the tests by teachers protesting at how they had increased their workload that the government brought in the idea of them being externally marked.

There was unease over the proposals with Eric Bolton, the chief schools inspector, warning that teachers should not allow politicians to take control of the national curriculum.

Heads, too, were already, pleading that enough was enough. "It is clear that heads are pretty tired of all the policy initiatives flying out of the Education Secretary's office – a sign that a June election is in the fray," wrote James Meikle, a colleague of mine at the *TES*, as he covered the Secondary Heads Association in April 1987, just one month before the UK went to the polls.

As for the NUT, they were also almost flummoxed by the stream of initiatives coming from the DES. Just before their conference, there was another one as the Education Secretary announced he wanted to devolve financial control of school budgets to headteachers. All secondary schools and primary schools with more than 200 pupils would have control by the early 1990s. It was based on a scheme piloted in Cambridgeshire and, on a simple level, it meant heads need no longer needed to wait for the local authority to act every time there was a leaking roof or faulty plumbing to repair.

The NUT's reaction to this was fairly predictable. By the time they got to their conference, they had seen their negotiating rights whittled away, and faced the prospect of a having a national curriculum imposed on them, and the beginnings – as they saw it – of the privatisation of the education system with the launch of the 20 business-sponsored City Technology Colleges. I wrote at the time that they knew how to oppose Sir Keith Joseph – they could "totally condemn" his "intransigence", "deplore" his failure to earmark more resources for the service and watch while he agonised over the future. The trouble with Kenneth Baker was that once they had condemned one initiative, he just moved on to the next one. One decision that the conference did take, though, was to call for "outright resistance" to the proposed tests for 7, 11 and 14-year-olds. Just what form that resistance would take, though, was unclear. The left favoured a boycott of any work to do with the tests – although there was a fear that, as they were to be the subject of legislation, teachers could be legally committed by their contract to carrying them out. Eric Bolton also took up the theme of the tests again, saying they could be "fraught with difficulties", adding that he did not want tests that would label children as failures from an early age or encourage teaching to the test at the expense of a broader curriculum – thus encapsulating the argument over the tests that was to run for the next two decades.

It was not long, though, before Mr Baker floated his next idea (all these initiatives were said to be about to form part of a general Bill to be introduced if the Conservatives retained power in the 1987 General Election). This was to allow schools to opt out of local authority control and receive their funding straight from Whitehall. Ostensibly, the idea was the forerunner of the current academies project – but at this stage it was seen as a recipe for successful schools – not an initiative that would help those struggling to serve disadvantaged communities. He promised that there would be no "backdoor selection" in opted-out schools – and they would be monitored by *him* to ensure they were not in any way reintroducing a type of 11-plus. While the CTCs would be free to opt out of the proposed new national curriculum so long as what they offered was "broadly consistent" with its values, the opted-out – or grant-maintained as was their official title – schools would have to abide by the national structure.

Within weeks of the election, Mr Baker's Great Education Rerform Bill (GERBIL) was published. True to form, it contained all the initiatives that he had rolled out so far: opting out, national curriculum, testing, local management of school budgets, the CTC programme. For good measure, there were also clauses on open enrolment – allowing popular schools to expand, charging for activities (although if it happened during the school day or was demanded by the curriculum, you couldn't charge) – and taking polytechnics and further education colleges out of local authority control. The government also set a date for the abolition of the ILEA and for the transfer of responsibility to the local boroughs – 1990. Among the GERBIL's opponents was former Conservative Prime Minister Edward Heath who said that Rab Butler – the architect of the 1944 Act which had largely shaped the current system of education – would be "turning in his grave". It was, he argued, "absolutely lamentable" to be allowing schools to charge for activities such as music.

There were hints of a difference of opinion between Mrs Thatcher and Mr Baker on opting out. She saw it being "as big as the one million transfer from the public sector (in housing) into owner-occupation" while he was insisting it would be no "let out" for schools facing closure because of reorganisation schemes. There were also signs of disagreement over the national curriculum with Mrs Thatcher wanting it to major on the basics and have them tested while Mr Baker, a man fond of reading and reciting poetry, favoured a broader and less utilitarian approach. Arts and drama were also included as foundation (core) subjects in the Bill. Mr Baker backed the idea of the National Curriculum taking up between 70 per cent and 80 per cent of the timetable, leaving schools freer to diversify for the rest of the time.

There was no denying it was one of the central planks of Mrs Thatcher's third term of office. She told the Conservative Party conference: "Our most important task in this Parliament is to raise the quality of education ... We want education to be part of the answer to Britain's problems, not the cause."

As far as Labour was concerned, Jack Straw, a former president of the National Union of Students, had now taken over from Giles Radice and trod a more pragmatic path than just outright opposition to the Bill. He honed in on the CTCs saying that, whilst Labour would not scrap them, it would want to see a return to local authority oversight.

Former Prime Minister James Callaghan, the man who had started the "great debate" on education a decade ago, weighed in against the Bill, too, describing Mr Baker as an "impetuous, able and ambitious minister in too much of a hurry". He was, in particular, hostile to the idea of schools opting out and the breaking up of the ILEA.

Mr Baker also had to deal with opposition from his two predecessors: Sir

Keith (now Lord) Joseph was worried about the prescriptive nature of the core curriculum and doubted the wisdom of continuous testing, while Lord Carlisle expressed concern about open enrolment, warning that it "does contain difficulties and is certainly expensive".

In the end, though, there were no major changes to the Bill as a result of its passage through Parliament and the GERBIL became the ERA (Education Reform Act) in July 1988.

*****

Rumbling on in the background at this time was the work of another government committee, headed by Professor Sir Gordon Higginson, to review A-levels. Professor Higginson's committee wanted to broaden the sixth-form curriculum and proposed that taking five A-levels should be the norm – in essence moving the exam towards the International Baccalaureate which was becoming increasingly popular in schools in the UK.

Professor Higginson was just one of many to fail to convince ministers of the need to broaden A-levels. They paid lip service to the idea but the argument against Higginson put forward by the government was that increasing the number to five would dilute the standard demanded in each subject. For a brief time, after the introduction of Curriculum 2000, we did adopt a slightly broader approach to A-levels with the introduction of the AS-level as a half A-level to be taken at the end of the first year in the sixth-form. The norm for pupils became taking four subjects at AS-level – then dropping their weakest suit after the AS-level exams. However, we have now reverted again to the three A-level mode as a result of Michael Gove's reforms, which decoupled the AS-level from the A-level. That led to many schools questioning the wisdom of continuing with AS-levels. Mr Gove's argument was that this would free the first year of the sixth-form up for pupils to develop a deeper understanding of their subject as they did not have to prepare for examinations at its end – a view I can have some sympathy with. However, there were howls of anguish in university circles – notably from Cambridge – which claimed it robbed them of seeing the only tangible efforts of a sixth-former's achievements before they had to decide whether to offer them a provisional place or not. It also diluted the breadth of the curriculum. With exams, as with many other reforms, it was a case of three steps forward followed by two steps backwards. We now have an examination system more reminiscent of the 1950s than the broader approach adopted by many of our European competitors.

*****

Of course, controversy over the Baker education reforms did not die with the passage of the Bill into law. An immediate challenge came in the form of schools planning to opt out as one of the first two aiming to go down this route had, in fact, been earmarked for closure by the local authority – Audenshaw in Tameside, Greater Manchester. The first school to be given the green light, though, was Skegness Grammar School (actually a comprehensive). Mr Baker, who had initially raised the spectre of opting out not being a bolt hole for those threatened with closure, also announced he was satisfied that Audenshaw had a future and gave it permission to become grant-maintained, too.

Meanwhile, the CTC initiative appeared to be floundering for want of sponsors. Sir Cyril Taylor, a former Conservative GLC alderman who had been appointed head of the CTC trust (and was later to become an adviser to Tony Blair's government), also warned that the initiative would fail if it concentrated on purchasing greenfield sites for them. That, he argued, would be much too costly. As a result, two schools in Lewisham, south London – the Haberdashers' Aske's single sex schools – were offered £4 million for refurbishment if parents agreed they should become CTCs. Not as costly as greenfield sites but costly enough to provoke claims from teachers' organisations that it was a "bribe" to ensure the success of the policy.

It was, however, time for an end to the Baker era (and an end to the zealous enthusiasm for the policy). His reward for his stewardship of the GERBIL through Parliament was to be given the job of chairman of the Conservative Party.

Thatcher's thinking was that she would like some breathing space for the reforms to bed down and she appointed John MacGregor – formerly with the Ministry of Agriculture, Fisheries and Food – with a view to ensure education remained in a safe pair of hands. His appointment had been greeted with assessments from former colleagues that he was "safe", "Conservative" and "unexciting" – just the man to preside over a period of stability within education. As if to emphasise his low-key approach, he said at the Conservative Party's local government conference that there would be no new school reforms until 1994 at the earliest. For good measure, in his private life he was an amateur conjuror – skills that could possibly have been very helpful to the government in the Sir Keith Joseph era. Unfortunately, from the view of many in the teaching profession, he did not last long enough to deliver this pledge. Pity the poor student given the task of writing a thesis about what John MacGregor had achieved in his time as Education Secretary. The answer would be nothing – not enough for two sides of foolscap.

Mr Baker's departure, though, led to valedictions claiming that his had been a successful reign. He had been good on policy presentation and had certainly achieved more in a short space of time than either of his predecessors. He had also wrong-footed Labour: Jack Straw, its education spokesman, was considered one of the bright lights of the shadow cabinet but he found himself too often in the position of having to react to the latest policy initiative than pursue his own agenda.

One of Mr Baker's last acts before leaving office was to pave the way for the introduction of student loans, which the government wanted to introduce in 1990. However, the NUS in particular mounted an effective campaign against the proposal – campaigning for a student boycott of any bank that became involved in operating the loans system. As many of them had a large number of student clients (many of whom were likely to stay with them for life), it created an atmosphere of unease. Four student unions – at Loughborough, York, Warwick and Bristol – were noticeably active in persuading their members to carry out the boycott. By December 1989, nine of the ten banks who had originally expressed an interest in the scheme had pulled out – and the government was forced into a corner whereby it would have to operate the scheme itself. It set up the Student Loans Company operating from Glasgow. Mrs Thatcher was said to be "fizzing with fury" over what she considered to be weakness and lack of backbone on the part of the banks – and threatened retribution of an unspecified nature. Jack Straw described this as her "Alice in Wonderland moment". "The Queen was in a furious passion and went stamping about and shouting 'off with his head' or 'off with her head' about once a minute," he said, paraphrasing Lewis Carroll.

Mrs Thatcher was so committed to the policy that, in an attempt to quash any backbench rebellion, she led the way through the lobby to vote on the proposal herself. In the end, only four Conservatives showed enough courage to vote against the proposal while 12 abstained – not enough to get the Commons to jettison it.

*****

By this time, I was becoming a bit restive after nine years at the *TES*. I kind of thought as I was approaching 40 that if I didn't leave now to join a national daily then I never would. The first offer that came my way was really out of the blue

– in more ways than one! I was headhunted by the *Daily Mail* – so much so that they sent one of their former education correspondents to take me out to lunch to try and convince me – in his words – that "It's not as bad as you might think". I have to confess to you I am not a natural ally of the *Daily Mail's* philosophy but I thought it was worth considering the offer. After all, two colleagues of mine, Stephen Bates and James Meikle, had worked there before going on to become successful education correspondents of *The Guardian*. I broached the subject with my wife, Anne, who, if anything, was probably less in sympathy with the *Mail's* view of things than me, and said I would think about it. It took me a week of avidly reading the paper from cover to cover before I decided it was not for me. I told Anne that night to be met with the response: "Oh, good, because I'd have divorced you if you'd accepted it." I'm not sure whether she was joking. She didn't look as though she was. Luckily, I never had to find out.

My second attempt at trying to get a job was at *The Independent*, a newcomer to the market, which at that stage had three education correspondents and took the subject very seriously. I was interviewed by John Price, its news editor, formerly of *The Times*, and subsequently told I would not be appointed – the reason being, according to the feedback I received, that I was considered to be too steeped in education. In other words, I would write boring tracts for those involved in the world of education but not spice them up enough for the daily newspaper market. (Subsequently, after I had secured my escape route through the *Mirror*, *The Independent* became a part of the Mirror group and we shared the same canteen. I met John Price one day and he smiled, adding: "I got you wrong.")

My third attempt was with *The Mirror* – I tried a different approach and sent a letter to the editor, Roy Greenslade, whom I had vaguely known earlier in my career. It was headed "ten reasons why you need an education correspondent". It featured ten stories about the savage impact that cuts were having on the education service which *The Mirror* had not covered. The lead item was the fact that around 500 children in Tower Hamlets were unable to go to school because there were not enough places for them.

The Mirror's response was to ask me to write them all up for them – to which my initial reaction was ****! I hadn't thought it through and how time consuming this would be! At any rate, a few days after I had completed the task *The Mirror* came out with one of its 'shock issues' – on education – featuring my stories and the picture of a six-year-old child from Tower Hamlets looking longingly through the railings of a school that he could not access.

The very day it appeared I received a telephone call from Roy Greenslade's office. Their current education correspondent, Charles Lyte, who also wrote about poetry and gardening, had taken early retirement and there was a vacancy. Could I pop in and see Roy that evening?

I arrived to find *The Mirror's* offices besieged by television cameras – they had just run a story about an alleged connection between Arthur Scargill and Libyan money at the height of the miners' strike. Any attempt at remaining incognito to any of the *TES* hierarchy who watched the news that night was effectively scuppered. I was ushered into Roy's office and asked not unnaturally why I wanted to work on *The Mirror.* "Well, I'm a left of centre journalist and you're a left of centre paper, I thought—" "Great," interrupted Roy, "You're hired. Now I'm a bit busy so I'll get my secretary to introduce you to people." I was introduced to Bill Hagerty, the deputy editor, and Steve Lynas, the news editor. I asked Steve about the paper. "Well, I'm a bit new here – this is my first day," he said. I left the office in a bit of a daze and rang up Anne. "I think I've been offered a job at *The Mirror,*" I said. "What do you mean think?!" "Well, there's been no talk of pay or starting dates but they did say they wanted me."

For the next four weeks I heard nothing and I thought it had all been a pipe dream. Then, at the NUT conference, Doug McAvoy, by then general secretary, gave a press briefing at 6pm, claiming that Militant was trying to seize control of the union. It made the lead in all the broadsheets and the page two lead in *The Sun.* Apparently the following day, a senior executive walked into Roy's office and said: "Who the **** was that guy who came in a few weeks ago and knew something about education?" Within minutes, *The Mirror* was on the phone to me, a contract was biked round (and signed and sent back) and the rest, as they say, is history.

*****

I realised I would have to adopt a more campaigning, racy style working for *The Mirror.* That much was obvious from the 'shock' issue prepared on the basis of the material I had submitted to Roy Greenslade before joining the paper – with its picture on the front page stating: "This boy is six and a half years old ... yet he started school only this term – 16 months late." It then delivered its verdict on Britain's education record: "Bottom of the Class". It probably helped that – for several years on the *TES* – I had specialised in covering the teachers' organisations who were in the best position to tell me about the impact of government cuts on the ground. The first story I wrote for them was from an interview with David Hart, then general secretary of the National Association of Head Teachers, warning that children may have to be sent home as a result of the cuts. He had sent a message to his 32,000 members saying: "Avoid teaching extra classes yourself, don't ask other staff to shoulder the burden and send pupils home if there are not enough teachers (because you can't afford to employ them)."

I soon realised that there was no shortage of people willing to supply information about the effect of cuts in spending in schools. One of them was Sir Claus Moser, former head of the government's statistical service who, in a speech as president of the British Association for the Advancement of Science, said millions of state school pupils were receiving an education "not worthy of a civilised society". In particular, he cited the appalling conditions of many school buildings – a campaign which *The Mirror* was to run with for several years.

Soon after his speech came the Conservative Party conference, which coincided with me being given details of a plan by Somerset County Council to scrap school meals. In future, it would only supply sandwiches for those children who were entitled to free school meals. We contrasted that with the three-course dinner on offer at the Conservatives' conference hotel.

We had a modest success with the campaign in the first year as the government set aside an extra £500 million to help schools cope with implementing the new national curriculum and repairing run-down classrooms. A bolder and brasher Richard Garner had emerged from the closet.

*****

John MacGregor was moved to become Leader of the Commons on leaving education and replaced by Kenneth Clarke. The feeling in the education world was that once again education was in the hands of a politician who was on the way up. The downside was that he had previously skirmished with the medical world and the health unions through presiding over cuts to the NHS budget during his time as Health Secretary. The comment by Nigel de Gruchy, general secretary of the NASUWT, to greet his arrival was hardly flattering: "If he does to education what he's doing to health then it will become a very sick service. It's worse than a joke." The other thought that came to mind was that Mr MacGregor's promise that there would be no new school reforms before 1994 at the earliest was unlikely to survive the arrival of someone trying to make their name in political circles.

Indeed, he did launch a few initiatives soon after arriving at the DES – implementing plans set out in the GERBIL for colleges (sixth-form and FE) to be taken out of local council control; and following on from Kenneth Baker's initiative on teachers' pay by formally setting up a pay review body for the teaching profession and launching an inquiry into teaching methods – with a view to phasing out mixed ability teaching in schools and replacing it with streaming or setting – the idea being that most teachers could not cope with teaching such a range of different abilities in one classroom. To this end, he set up a review of primary education.

Mr Clarke quite often shot from the hip – which could get him into trouble. He gave an interview in April, 1991 in which he was quoted as saying: "I have never met anyone who did not want to send their children into independent schools if they could afford it. I know some of my political opponents like to say they sent their children to state schools. But in most cases I regard that as hypocrisy or sacrificing their children to promote their political career." Questioned about the comments – published in *The Mirror* – in the Commons by Labour's Jack Straw he claimed the paper was read by "morons". That, of course, was red rag to a bull for our editor Richard Stott who then ran a poll in *The Mirror* asking our readers to decide whether Mr Clarke himself was a moron – or just a prat. It can hardly be coincidence that, just after this episode, I went through a period of not being informed about government-organised press briefings on education (don't worry, I was always told about them by colleagues and just turned up and nothing was said). I did decide to raise it with a senior press officer at one point only to be told: "Let's face it, Richard, you're hardly our number one priority." I did point out that our readers were taxpayers just like any others. This sort of treatment was never meted out to representatives of the *Mail* and *Telegraph* when Labour was in office.

Another flashpoint came during the Conservative Party conference when I accompanied Mr Clarke on a school visit to open a new £800,000 school complex at Fleetwood High School just outside Blackpool. We were in the school library when I started questioning him about the lack of resources for school buildings generally – a school down the road had temporary classrooms installed after the Second World War which had not yet been replaced. I suddenly became aware that the photographer accompanying me was snapping away furiously. It transpired the word 'Fiction' could be seen displayed above his head.

I digress, though. There were other initiatives launched during Kenneth Clarke's period of office which were of lasting quality. He set in motion plans to set up the new education standards watchdog, Ofsted, which would take over responsibility for inspecting the nation's state schools. It was to be a far more robust system than the previous regime run by HMI – delivering pass or fail verdicts on schools and, at one time, ranking individual teachers on a scale of one to seven. However, ever since its inception, it has managed to maintain an independence from government, showing no fear or favour in its criticisms. Plans for exam league tables were also drawn up in this period, giving the GCSE and A-level results of every school in the country and their truancy records. Both initiatives were key factors behind the new target-driven approach adopted by schools, which teachers complained left them with little time to adopt their own initiatives in the classroom.

*****

Soon after Kenneth Clarke took over at the DES, there was a far bigger upheaval in the running of the country – Margaret Thatcher resigned to be replaced by John Major. In his first comments on education after taking office, Mr Major talked about his vision of the "classless" society and of raising the pay and status of teachers. Labour, though, had its own vision of the "class-*less*" society where teachers had to take classes in halls or corridors because the existing classrooms were too damp or overcrowded.

At this stage, one statistic that was often trotted out was the fact that the UK had far fewer pupils staying on in education after the age of 16 than almost any other country in Europe and Mr Major made it part of his brief to come up with ideas to combat this – one of which was to propose training credits of £1,000 to young people who did decide to stay on. (This eventually came to fruition with the education maintenance allowances of up to £30 a week offered under Labour after it succeeded to office in 1997.) Mr Major also pushed ahead with the idea of abolishing the distinction between polytechnics and universities as part of an attempt to give more esteem to the more skills-based courses offered in polytechnics. Unfortunately, though, what on the face of it seemed a good egalitarian idea floundered as many of the former polytechnics adopted a policy of aping the existing universities – and offering a more academic diet to their pupils.

During the 18 months he was Prime Minister before the 1992 General Election, Mr Major also saw the resignation of Eric Bolton, Chief Inspector of Schools under the old HMI regime. Mr Bolton said he wanted to go to give himself more freedom to speak out about what he saw in education. (That may seem odd to those whose vision of inspectors conjures up images of Chris Woodhead and Sir Michael Wilshaw – but the HMI service was a much more cautious animal than Ofsted came to be.) He did, however, practise some of that freedom before he left office, referring in a farewell briefing for education correspondents to the "stubborn" statistic that 30 per cent of schools were still providing a poor standard of education for their children. *The Mirror* ran the story as a front page lead. "Good God," said editor Richard Stott, "what's he going to come up with if he wants more freedom to speak out?"

TIMELINE

1987

Kenneth Baker publishes GERBIL, introducing National Curriculum and tests for 7, 11 and 14-year-olds as well as policy of allowing schools to opt out of council control and be funded directly by Whitehall plus the establishment of a network of City Technology Colleges. Bill also backs open enrolment – allowing popular schools to expand – and charging for non-national curriculum activities outside of school hours.

Review of A-levels by Professor Sir Gordon Higginson recommends five A-levels should be the norm for sixth-formers.

1988

Government announces it is seeking abolition of ILEA.

Figures show the International Baccalaureate is becoming more popular as an alternative to A-levels in UK schools – expected to rise from 12,600 students in 1986 to 20,000 by the end of the decade.

Government turns down Higginson report, fearing it would lead to reduced standards.

The GERBIL becomes law with few amendments.

First GCSE results revealed – exam boards publish national picture for first time.

Proposal for top-up loans for university students introduced in Commons.

1989

First schools – Skegness Grammar and Audenshaw – opt out of council control.

Elton report on school discipline published. It says the belief of teachers that smaller classes could help deal with discipline was "impressive and could not be ignored".

John MacGregor takes over from Kenneth Baker as Education Secretary.

Banks withdraw support for the student loans scheme and the Student Loans Company is set up to mastermind it.

1990

Student loans legislation passed.

ILEA abolished – with power to run education resorting to individual boroughs.

Kenneth Clarke takes over from John MacGregor.

1991

Kenneth Clarke sets up independent pay review body for teachers.

Proposals to abolish the distinction between polytechnics and universities published.

Chapter Four
The Major Years

John Patten was the man chosen to take on the education mantle when the Conservatives won a surprising victory in the 1992 election – surprising, that was, to the pollsters who even in the exit poll were predicting a hung Parliament. (Subsequent elections have shown perhaps we should not be surprised that the pollsters got it wrong, though.)

At first sight, Mr Patten, an Oxford MP, appeared to have one or two things going for him. His daughter, Mary Claire, aged five, attended a state school – St Vincent de Paul primary in Westminster. It made him the first holder of his office since the Conservatives regained power in 1979 to have a child going through the state education system.

His appointment took most pundits aback. He had been a junior minister in the previous administration for several years and was not thought of as a high-flyer. Indeed, there were some who suggested that whoever had called on John Major's behalf to offer him the post had dialled the wrong number – and had been meant to offer the job to Chris Patten, a former Schools Minister who later became chairman of the party and director general of the BBC, and who had been tipped for high office by most observers.

At any rate, it seemed to suggest that education would not be at the centre of the government's endeavours – unlike the position it had held under Kenneth Baker and, to a lesser extent, Kenneth Clarke. John Patten's in-tray would have told him that his major job was overseeing the school reforms initiated under the previous administration.

Top of this list was encouraging schools to opt out of local authority control. A White Paper on education published just three months after the election victory laid out a vision of every school having opted out of council control by the end of the decade. In essence, opting out was the forerunner of academisation. The structure was similar – the schools would be given the green light to run themselves in the same way as those in the private sector did. The vision may have been the same but the method of achieving it was very different. There was no compulsion, and there had to be a ballot of parents before any action was taken. As a result, it did not attract the wrath of backbench MPs in the same way as, two decades later, David Cameron's plan to force schools to become academies.

John Patten himself was gung-ho about the policy. In a rash speech to the Conservative Party conference which would probably be described nowadays as a 'Gary Lineker moment', he promised to "eat his hat with garnish" (at least he didn't promise to appear on TV in his underwear) if half the nation's schools had not opted out by the time of the next election.

A report published by Local Schools Information two years into the government's term of office said this target would not be reached, even though there had been initial enthusiasm for the new structure. By 1994, 926 schools had opted out but, in the latest school term, the number of new applications had trickled down to just 30. (*The Mirror* did offer him the opportunity to carry out his pledge – even supplying the hat! – but he declined.) Of course, one of the reasons why schools became more reluctant to opt out may have been the pledge by Labour to abolish opt-out status – causing some heads to wonder what would be the point in securing the new structure if they only had to revert back to something akin to local authority control if Labour won the next election.

A second major reform that Mr Patten presided over was the introduction of secondary school performance tables, whereby schools had to publish their exam results and truancy records so parents could compare them in making up their minds about which school to choose for their offspring.

Unsurprisingly, the schools at the bottom of the league tables largely served run-down inner city areas. We at *The Mirror* focused on one in Gravesend, Kent – Southfields High – where only one per cent of pupils achieved the benchmark of five A to C grades at GCSE. It had the added disadvantage that, although comprehensive in name, it served an area which retained grammar schools. In effect, therefore, it was a secondary modern, missing out on the cream of the talented pupils. Many of its 11-year-olds arrived at the school with a reading age of just six.

The Mirror had decided not to publish the league tables on the grounds that we did not think the information the schools had to give painted a complete picture of what they had achieved. I have to say, though, that when I collected the information to write a story about the tables, I found my desk surrounded by senior executives of the paper who wanted to see how their child's school had performed. I thought then – and still do now – that if they created that much interest even amongst people who might have been opposed to their publication, they were here to stay. You can give parents information but it is politically tricky to take it away. The next year, therefore, we published the league tables. I found that, in years to come, there were in fact interesting stories to be found about schools which had bucked the trend – succeeding in achieving good exam results despite battling against disadvantage. In the end, you could argue that, by thrusting the spotlight on this, the tables helped struggling schools to identify others in the neighbourhood who could give them useful tips on how they could improve their performance. Some good could come of the league tables if you were prepared to put in the effort and work at it.

The third strand of the school reform legacy that John Patten had to cope with was the introduction of National Curriculum tests for 7, 11 and 14-year-olds. One of the main objections by teachers' leaders to the new regime was that it would encourage schools to "teach to the tests" and thus limit pupils' access to a broad primary school curriculum. Conservative-controlled Wandsworth Council decided to take legal action to stop the boycott but lost its case when the NASUWT, one of the unions involved in the action, argued it was an issue centring around teachers' workload: the marking of the tests imposed a heavy and unmanageable burden on teachers. In the end, there was a victory of sorts for the teachers in that the demands of the tests were slimmed down – they would concentrate on testing the basics. The workload was eased as the tests for 11-year-olds were to be externally marked, although, ironically, this bestowed upon them an even greater importance than before and, it could be argued, that put more pressure on teachers to reach targets.

Away from the school reforms he had inherited, Mr Patten did introduce his own initiative – to set up a "Mum's Army" of classroom assistants who would go into schools as teaching assistants and train on the job to be teachers. It floundered, though, because of a threat by the teachers' unions to boycott the scheme – on the grounds that the training on offer would not be adequate for them to take control of a class.

While John Patten was struggling to implement the school reforms he had inherited, he soon lost any advantage that he had gained by having his daughter educated in the state sector by snubbing conference after conference. In one of his first acts on taking office, he decided against going to the National Association of Head Teachers' annual conference – saying that he was still reading in on his brief. When he turned down an invitation to the North of England Education Conference eight months later (the fifth time he had refused an invitation to a major education conference) the education world had had enough. "Please respond to those working in education and find out what is going on," said Ken Watson, a Conservative local authority leader from Devon. They dubbed him the 'Invisible Man' – a theme *The Mirror* was happy to exploit with a picture of him swathed in bandages. It was an epithet which stuck to him for the rest of his period in office.

He did have a habit of putting his foot in it, too – most notably over the launch of a discipline document which called for schools to only use exclusion as a last resort and to open more centres specialising in teaching disruptive pupils. He chose the occasion to reveal that he had been flogged twice by monks at his school, Wimbledon College, a Catholic secondary school in south London, once for forgetting a maths theorem. The end result was that the document on discipline received scant publicity while cohorts of distinguished journalists were despatched to find the monk who had flogged the Secretary of State. They failed.

The story I remember most vividly about his time in office, though, stemmed from his department's move to swanky new offices – Sanctuary Buildings in Great Smith Street, Westminster. The offices, which cost £12 million to rent at a time when schools were having to cope with austerity cuts, harboured an atrium with foliage cascading down to a marble floor at ground level. We did a story highlighting the difference between these offices and the conditions in which many teachers had to work. The following day I received a telephone call from someone who identified himself as a civil servant. Oh no, I thought, and mentally prepared myself to receive a tirade of abuse. "Congratulations on your story today," said the voice on the other end of the phone, "but there's one thing you missed out." "Oh?" "Yes, the spiders." "The spiders?" I queried. "Yes," said the civil servant. "There are so many greenfly inhabiting his hanging garden that they have to buy in spiders every month to kill them off." I tried to question him about how much this all cost but he hung up, saying: "I've said enough." So I rang a number of firms supplying pest control and – at the sixth port of call – a man responded: "Oh, you mean the Sanctuary Buildings contract?" However, he then clammed up and cited client confidentiality about revealing any details of the contract. Nevertheless, we were able to run a story about how the department was having to buy in thousands of spiders, blackflies and even wasps every month to control the greenfly. "I'm glad he's found a way to deal with the problem," said Doug McAvoy, general secretary of the NUT. "Perhaps he can turn his mind to something more pressing now." It was not, of course, John Patten's fault but it was the sort of thing that happens to a hapless minister.

John Patten was eventually sacked by John Major in the summer of 1994. Just before he left office, his former senior civil servant, Sir Geoffrey Holland, who was Permanent Secretary at the Department for Education (it had undergone a name change in the Patten era – it was now the Department *for* Education rather than the Department *of* Education and Science because Mr Patten thought that gave out a more positive image), spoke out against the state of the education service in Britain. There was not much positive in what he had to say. "I have a very haunted feeling that time is running out for us to compete as a nation. The drop out rate from education is too high. Standards across the board are still too low. They are lower than they should be if we are to hold a candle to emerging countries in the Far East like Japan, Taiwan and India."

If anything, John Patten's reign as Education Secretary was living proof that constant reform of the education system was turning it into a battlefield. He was heading towards defeat in meeting the objectives he had set himself on the number of schools that opted out of local council control; he had found himself at the centre of another industrial dispute with the teachers' unions over testing; and he was under fire for presiding over the introduction of the system that was designed to put a check on teaching standards: the publication of performance tables and the creation of the education standards watchdog, Ofsted, with its regular inspections of every state school in the land. Yet, when he left office, it appeared he had accomplished little. Apparently, on the day that he was called in by John Major to be relieved of his post, he believed he was going to be congratulated about the job he was doing. Nothing could be further from the truth, it transpired.

*****

If anything, the background of Mr Patten's successor – Gillian Shephard – would have been even more reassuring to those in the teaching profession than her predecessor. After all, she had in fact been a teacher herself before moving to become an education inspector with Norfolk County Council. She was moved to the job from the Ministry of Agriculture, Fisheries and Food and was viewed as a politician who was on the way up – and perhaps a safer pair of hands than her predecessor.

One of the issues that dominated her reign actually had its genesis before she was appointed to the office of Secretary of State. Sir Claus Moser, former head of the government's statistical service, had been appointed to head the

National Commission on education – an inquiry funded by the Paul Hamlyn Foundation – after a call for a Royal Commission of Inquiry into the education system had been rejected. His report did not pull its punches. One of the key recommendations was that all children should have the chance to start nursery schooling at the age of three. "Nursery education from three onwards would be a major factor in cutting down on crime, delinquency and hooliganism later in life," said Sir Claus. "And I don't just mean playing. I mean proper nursery education – giving children a start to learn the basic skills ... we believe we should phase it in over a number of years and set specific targets, concentrating on children in deprived areas first." Controversially, Sir Claus's report recommended that *less* money should be spent on higher education, while the resources saved should be devoted to the early years of education. It was, in fact, a seminal report which not only paved the way for universal nursery education but added impetus to the idea that students should pay more towards the cost of their university courses.

Sir Claus is widely credited with convincing Prime Minister John Major of the need to give nursery education a priority. It was then, though, that ideology played a hand. The government wanted to introduce a voucher scheme for its introduction. Under it, parents of four-year-olds – as a first step – would be given vouchers of £1,100 a year to spend at the institution of their choice: it could be a nursery school, day nursery or playgroup. However, critics argued that the scheme would take away money from local authorities who were already offering nursery places. They would only get it back if sufficient numbers of parents chose to send their children to them. A further complication was that the scheme envisaged only offering the vouchers to parents of four-year-olds – thus threatening provision already in place for three-year-olds. Just before the election in 1997 – and just before the voucher scheme was due to go nationwide on April 1 that year – a draft report on the scheme from the Conservative-dominated Commons select committee on education was leaked to *The Mirror* claiming that the scheme was "wasteful" and "pointless". Money would be spent on administering the scheme which could be spent on provision.

During her tenure as Education Secretary, Gillian Shephard also had to cope with evidence of a rising tide of indiscipline in schools. Addressing the NAHT conference after it had revealed that the number of pupils being excluded from school had trebled in three years to more than 10,000 a year, she promised there would be a government review of school discipline and the sanctions available to teachers.

The issue was to dog the headlines over the rest of her period in charge with the worst example occurring at the Ridings School in Halifax where members of the

NASUWT had drawn up a list of 60 unruly children whom they would refuse to teach. The union was asking for them to be excluded from school. Later the situation escalated and the school had to be closed down for a few days after two boys sexually assaulted a teacher. Mrs Shephard warned the school that it would be taken over by a government-appointed "hit squad" if it did not sort itself out – and Ofsted was sent in to carry out an emergency inspection of the school. The idea of sending a "hit squad" into a school to turn it round had been tried out for the first time at Hackney Downs school in north London – a once flourishing grammar school which numbered actor Michael Caine as one of its alumni. It had, however, fallen upon hard times with very few parents wanting to send their children to the school, almost one in five of those who were on the roll playing truant and only a handful of pupils obtaining the benchmark five A to C grades at GCSE. That intervention, of course, eventually paid off with Hackney Downs closing and Mossbourne Academy opening on the same site under the headship of Sir Michael Wilshaw, later to become the nation's chief schools inspector and who notched up an enviable record of getting pupils into Oxbridge while he was at the school. The Ridings, though, was not so fortunate. Sir Mike Tomlinson, who headed the inspection team that went into the school (and who later become chief schools inspector), described it as the worst school he had ever seen for discipline problems. It flourished for a while under a new head, Anna White, but in the end had to be closed. The odds were stacked against it: it was the only school in the area that was not either a grammar or a faith school, and few people chose to send their children to it.

As for the attempts to improve discipline in school, they remained high on the agenda politically for several years, with Labour appointing a discipline 'tsar' when it came to office. Guidance to teachers on how to deal with potentially violent situations was amended to allow them to use reasonable force to control the situation. The NASUWT, which was the main teachers' organisation to be campaigning on the issue, focused on how appeals panels often let back into school unruly pupils who had been expelled by the head – as in the case of a 13-year-old pupil at Glaisdale School in Nottinghamshire who had a list of 45 incidents of indiscipline recorded against him. The union's strategy of refusing to teach a pupil in such circumstances was memorably described by its general secretary as "industrial action with a halo" – it was intended to improve discipline in the classroom, and it did win significant concessions in cutting down the number of times pupils excluded for violence were returned by appeals panel to the scene of their crimes.

(Of course, the two saddest incidents of violence in schools during that period wreaked much more havoc than classroom indiscipline – the murder of respected headteacher Philip Lawrence as he was attacked by a youth with a machete going to protect a boy outside his school gates at St George's, Maida Vale in 1995; and the Dunblane massacre where scout master Thomas Hamilton went on the rampage and slaughtered children in the town's primary school in 1996. There is no sure and fast recipe for dealing with such situations.)

As the next election loomed large on the horizon, the spotlight inevitably turned to what would be in the party manifestos, and there were rumours of a difference of opinion between Mr Major and Mrs Shephard on the content. John Major was anxious to see a return to selection and wanted to campaign on the motto "a grammar school in every town". Mrs Shephard, whose original speech at the venue where the initiative was launched made no mention of the idea, said schools would be able to select bright pupils – even if the local education authority opposed the idea.

The opinion polls were pointing to a substantial Labour victory and Mrs Shephard's last act before the election was to address the NASUWT conference where she told teachers she hoped to be back to see them the following year. Mr de Gruchy said she would be welcome but added that she might be "a shadow of her former self".

Of course, the Conservatives were defeated at the 1997 election and Mrs Shephard did not stay long in her education brief after the defeat. Her three years in office had been characterised by efficient administration, reacting sensibly to crises such as The Ridings School, and there were none of the gaffes of the Patten regime. Towards the end, though, there was a sense of biding time until a new administration took over.

*****

Labour, meanwhile, was busy preparing a credible alternative education policy to the government's in advance of the General Election. It was obvious that education was going to be top of its agenda even before party leader Tony Blair declared his top three priorities were going to be "education, education, education".

The first policy document published by Labour after Mr Blair's election as party leader was on education and he appeared at the launch to give his take on the recommendations.

It was obvious within minutes that there was to be a new emphasis, which he was later to describe in an interview with me after becoming Prime Minister as the "carrot and stick" approach. The stick was very much in evidence at the launch as he seized on one of the recommendations – to set up a General Teaching Council along the lines of the General Medical Council – to safeguard standards in the profession. Mr Blair sought to interpret it as a means to weed out and get rid of bad teachers. "It will make sure teachers uphold the highest standards," he said. "Those who prove unfit to do the job of good teaching should be removed." The other area he highlighted from the document was getting parents to sign home-school contracts – pledging to do all within their power to make sure homework was delivered on time and there was no truanting.

Other recommendations in the document included replacing A-levels with a baccalaureate type of exam which would ensure sixth-formers took a broader range of studies than just the traditional A-levels; and a pledge to get rid of exam league tables. There was no highlighting of these in Mr Blair's speech. One got the feeling the approach would be very different if Labour's Shadow Education Secretary, Ann Taylor, had been left to her own devices.

Within three months, Ann Taylor had been replaced as shadow spokesperson by David Blunkett who wasted no time in outlining his blueprint for the future. In his first interview with me he stressed: "Mediocrity will not be tolerated." Raising standards was to be at the forefront of every policy initiative and, to this end, teacher training would be reformed to put more emphasis on how to teach numeracy and literacy and on keeping control of the class. Opt-out status for schools would be abolished and they would return to the local authority fold (albeit with the proviso that they could appoint their own foundation governors) and exam tables, instead of being abolished, would be used more positively to highlight those schools which had improved their results. Nursery provision would be improved and there would more effective use of pupil referral units to teach excluded children.

He next turned his attention to failing schools and unveiled the 'Fresh Start' initiative, under which a persistently failing school would be closed down and opened up with a new name, new headteacher and quite possibly new teaching staff. "The new school, with a new governing body, a new headteacher and new teachers would be able to offer pupils a fresh chance of success," he said. Not surprisingly, though, the idea of sacking teachers raised the hackles of union leaders with Peter Smith, general secretary of the normally moderate Association of Teachers and Lecturers, commenting: "Mr Blunkett is suggesting mass murder when only a surgical strike is needed." The teachers' opposition to the scheme was taken on to a different plane when Mr Blunkett arrived to address the annual conference of the NUT at Blackpool that Easter. Demonstrators were waiting to greet him outside the Winter Gardens and chased him across the foyer, hurling insults at him and eventually cornering him outside an office. Stewards helped him to barricade inside while the barrage continued in full view of the television cameras. The office was referred to as a cupboard in some sections of the media which, whilst not accurate, might give you an indication of how much space there was in it. He remained inside for about half an hour until Doug McAvoy, general secretary of the union, arrived and pleaded with the demonstrators to disperse. Having secured maximum television coverage by then, they did so. The demonstrators were also reacting to a leak of the speech he intended to give to the conference later on in the day which said he would urge teachers not to strike over education cuts. Mr McAvoy was forthright in his condemnation of them saying the whole episode must have been "a terrifying experience". If it was, it did not seem to affect Mr Blunkett as he robustly addressed the conference later on that day.

(The episode had an interesting sequel the following year when Mr Blunkett's advisers ushered him in through a back entrance to the Cardiff conference centre to avoid any repeat of the demonstration. Sharp-eyed BBC Education Correspondent Mike Baker noticed him coming in via the rear entrance and rushed up to him, microphone in hand, to ask why he was using the back entrance. "I don't know this is the ***** back entrance," came the reply. "It's just where they told me to go." Later in the week he was given a standing ovation from the NASUWT conference – in marked contrast to the NUT – when he promised them a 10-year investment programme for education.

He later fleshed out his education policy further by outlining a plan for a new "superteacher" pay grade to try and encourage the best teachers to stay in the classroom rather than accept a management role as the only way to boost their pay. In addition, he proposed setting a minimum amount of time for homework for each year group. Each school was also to set targets for improving their exam results.

Labour was thrown off course, though, at the beginning of 1996 when it was revealed that Harriet Harman, one of Mr Blunkett's fellow shadow cabinet members, was sending her son to a grammar school outside the area that they lived in. Indeed, she had to cross five Labour-controlled local education authority areas in the journey to her son's new school. The party was opposed to the 11-plus – indeed Tony Blair confirmed this in speeches – and in the 1997 election campaign was to put forward a proposal giving parents the right to ballot on ending grammar school status if they so wished. Ms Harman's situation was an embarrassment to David Blunkett who had focused on trying to improve standards in the comprehensive system. My memory of that incident is being called in by Piers Morgan (by then editor of *The Mirror*) along with

David Seymour, chief leader writer at *The Mirror,* and Fiona Wyton, deputy editor, to hear Piers giving a blunt ultimatum: "We can't duck this issue. Either we've got to say Labour policy is all wrong and they should drop their opposition to grammar schools – or we criticise Harriet Harman for a flagrant breach of Labour Party policy." I recall saying something about my opposition to the 11-plus and that it blighted children's lives and that I in no way would like to see it being extended. David Seymour then weighed in with: "Look, Piers, I think we have to remember our readership is more left-wing than we are and they would not tolerate us supporting grammar schools." Piers Morgan screwed up his eyes in disbelief: "What? They're more left wing than the three of you? God save us." He heeded the message, though, and we opted to back Labour in its attempt to revitalise the comprehensive system and criticise Harriet Harman for her decision.

And so to the manifesto. Labour had already drawn up its five key pledges for the election campaign – one of which was to introduce legislation outlawing class sizes of more than 30 for five to seven-year-olds. This would be the first act of the incoming government and it was to be paid for by abolishing the Assisted Places Scheme, where bright pupils from poor backgrounds in state schools were granted subsidised places at independent schools. It was a straightforward ideological decision: money should be given to improving conditions in the state sector rather than to subsidising some of the country's best-known private schools. Most of the ideas that David Blunkett had talked about in the run-up to the launch of the election were there, too: "superteachers" to be paid extra to remain the classroom, an end to opt-out status, and a boost in the number of pupil referral units for excluded pupils. There were a few extras, too: more cash for schools that opted to specialise in a particular subject area, and an encouragement to more schools to adopt setting (putting pupils in different ability groups for different subject areas). The accent was very much on setting rather than streaming, where pupils were put in the same stream for all subject areas. I had been a victim of this at school: I was put in the top stream because I had shown some ability in English and maths. I had shown no ability whatsoever in science subjects and floundered hopelessly as I tried to make my way in them in the top set. Flesh was put on the bones of the "superteacher" policy in that areas with a large cluster of underperforming schools, *ie* those that had failed their Ofsted report, were to be placed in "action zones" where incentives would be offered to recruit the best teachers to them.

One thing that was not tackled, though, was student finance, which would await the outcome of an inquiry being conducted by Sir Ron Dearing – the man who had got the Conservative government out of a hole on its national curriculum and testing plans by recommending a slimmed down version of them to schools. There was all-party consensus on setting up the inquiry, which was to report after the election, thus relieving the politicians from having to declare themselves on this issue during the campaign.

*****

It was not just the politicians who were making a name for themselves in the education world during the Major era. Step forward Chris Woodhead, who became Chief Inspector of Schools and head of the new education standards watchdog Ofsted in 1994.

Woodhead was another who started as he meant to go on, telling the *Daily Mail* in his first week of office that there were 15,000 incompetent teachers in schools and he was determined to weed them out. The tougher inspection regime, with every state school inspected every four years, gave him an opportunity to point out the weaknesses in the system.

He was a firm believer in "traditional" teaching methods by the time he took up the Ofsted job and had little time for "progressive" education theories. Some suggested this had not always been the case. One of his former teaching colleagues at Gordano school in Bristol told the ATL conference that he had been a classroom "trendy", teaching his English pupils about modern novels rather than Shakespeare.

Mr Woodhead repeated the "15,000 incompetent teachers" message when he published his annual report in February 1996. It also claimed that half the nation's primary schools and two out of every five secondary schools were failing to deliver a decent standard of education – and that one in five lessons were poorly delivered. It added that 3,000 primary schools were housed in dilapidated buildings, as were 800 secondary schools. A total of 1,400 primary schools and 300 secondary schools also did not have enough textbooks to deliver the National Curriculum.

Mr Woodhead said of those teachers considered not to be up to the job: "These teachers damage the education of children and undermine the work of their colleagues. It is in nobody's interests for them to remain in the profession."

His comments obviously reflected badly on the government – the Conservatives had been in power for 17 years and could not legitimately blame anyone else. It was rather ironic that Mr Woodhead was dismissed as a right-wing ideologue by many in the teaching profession when his comments provided no comfort for the Conservative administration. Perhaps, though, he was speaking out without fear or favour and doing what he considered his job to be – pointing out the defaults in the state education system whoever was responsible for them.

Later that year he went on to publish a report about reading standards in inner city schools – inspectors surveyed Islington, Southwark and Tower Hamlets – which showed that as many as eight out of ten pupils were behind in reading by the age of seven. By the time they transferred to secondary school, they could be as much as four years behind in reading.

Tower Hamlets was to remedy this in spectacular fashion over the ensuing years – getting to the point where its results in English tests for 11-year-olds were better than those of Kent, despite the fact that more than half the primary school population only spoke English as a second language.

One of the stories which stands out to me during my career on *The Mirror* came from an Ofsted report which – after the reading report – lavished praise on the 300 teachers hired by Tower Hamlets to help children with their reading under a scheme that gave extra cash to councils for teaching those whose first language was not English. Within weeks of the report, the government had axed the grant that provided the funding – so their jobs were under threat. The headline to the story summed the situation up: "Q. What reward will 300 brilliant teachers get for giving deprived youngsters a chance in life? A: The sack." A few weeks later, we heard that the government had reversed its decision to axe the funding although it was stressed to me this decision was in no way related to the article I had written. I didn't believe that.

Meanwhile, Mr Woodhead continued with his campaign to identify weaknesses in the system. By this time, Ofsted and the way it conducted its affairs had become a number one policy issue for the teachers' organisations – with regular calls for it to be wound up (and no-confidence motions in Mr Woodhead) on the grounds that it was placing too much stress on teachers and that it concentrated too much on the negative and ignored the positive.

In his annual report in the election year, he drew attention to incompetent headteachers, saying that 3,000 of them lacked the ability to do the job properly. His claim was immediately followed by a pledge from David Blunkett to train potential headteachers in leadership skills. Weak leadership skills, the chief inspector argued, was one of the most important problems to tackle.

Meanwhile, expectations were building up in the teaching world that Mr Woodhead would lose his job if Labour were elected – not something that Tony Blair or David Blunkett encouraged. Questions were also raised as to whether – because of his convictions – he would be prepared to work with Labour. He reassured everyone on that score. "I see no problem with working with Labour," he told me in an interview. "Labour has focused positively on key issues which have emerged from our school inspections. Both Tony Blair and David Blunkett have spoken very forcefully of the need for a tough external inspection system for schools." It was no surprise, then, that he survived the change of government.

TIMELINE

1992

John Patten takes over as Education Secretary.

Ofsted inspection system comes into being.

First exam league tables published.

Government sets target of all schools opting out of council control within a decade.

1993

Teachers vote to boycott tests for 7, 11 and 14-year-olds, leading to them winning concessions on slimming down the tests.

John Patten booed and hissed at NAHT conference and refuses to take questions.

National Commission on Education recommends every three-year-old should have access to a nursery place.

1994

John Patten is replaced by Gillian Shephard.

David Blunkett takes over as Shadow Education Secretary and promises big expansion of nursery school places.

1995

Blunkett unveils 'Fresh Start' scheme whereby failing schools are closed down and reopened with a new name and new staff. He is forced to take refuge in an office to escape demonstrators hounding him at NUT conference.

Government unveils nursery voucher scheme, whereby parents are given £1,100 a year to buy a place at the institution of their choice.

Hackney Downs becomes the first school to be taken over by a government "hit squad" because of poor performance.

Headteacher Philip Lawrence murdered by machete-wielding youth outside his school gates.

1996

John Major and Gillian Shephard launch "grammar school in every town" initiative as precursor to General Election.

Teachers at the Ridings School in Halifax draw up a hit list of 60 pupils they want excluded – or they go on strike.

Scoutmaster Thomas Hamilton kills 16 children and a teacher with a teacher at Dunblane Primary School.

1997

Nursery voucher scheme comes into force despite warning in leaked Commons select committee draft report that it will not raise standards, widen choice for parents or improve nursery provision.

Tony Blair goes to the country with "education, education, education" as his top three priorities.

Chapter Five
Education, education, education

Labour hit the ground running with its education reforms once it had secured a massive victory in the 1997 election – as one would have expected from a party whose leader had promised "education, education, education" would be his top three priorities.

First off the statute book was legislation to outlaw class sizes of more than 30 for all five to seven-year-olds – the measure to be paid for by stopping the £120 million a year spent on the Assisted Places Scheme. Opponents of the measure claimed its demise would rob disadvantaged pupils of the chance of going to the country's top private schools but, in the end, the death of the controversial scheme paved the way for many of the schools involved in it to increase the numbers of scholarships and bursaries that were on offer. Talk of a more robust approach on the part of the Charities Commission, in investigating whether the schools concerned were abiding by their founders' desire to provide education for the poor, may just have played a part in this.

As for the reduction in class sizes, it was one of the five key pledges made by Labour during the election campaign and dutifully carried through. However, many in the education world hoped it would be a precursor to reducing class sizes in other parts of the education sector, say for seven to 11-year-olds, or making further inroads into class sizes for infants. That never happened. Academic research – especially from Tennessee in the United States – found that reduced class sizes only had a real impact if there was a major reduction (from 30 to 14, for argument's sake). Otherwise, the effect on standards was minimal.

In its first month in office, there was plenty more about education in the Queen's Speech: setting up a General Teaching Council which was sold to the public on the basis that it would have powers to sack incompetent teachers; implementing the 'Fresh Start' initiative; and getting all local education authorities to set targets for improvements in exam and tests results – and holding over them the threat of being taken over by a team of experts if they failed to reach them.

In addition, the government set its own target of 80 per cent of pupils to reach the required standard in reading in national curriculum tests for 11-year-olds in the lifetime of the current Parliament (assuming it went its five years to 2002) and 75 per cent to reach the standard in maths. At the time the targets were set the figures were 57 and 55 per cent respectively. (It was easier to portray this, in laymen's eyes, as getting 80 per cent of pupils to pass the reading tests but, in actual fact, the tests set a standard that 11-year-olds should attain. It was based on the average performance of 11-year-olds when the tests were first mooted – and was always open for misinterpretation.)

David Blunkett acknowledged that the targets were ambitious but said: "No one should doubt that we mean business when we say education, education and education – and that behind that determination is standards, standards, standards."

Judging by historical standards, the aim was ambitious. According to research published by the highly respected National Foundation for Educational Research, there had been no improvement in reading standards since the Second World War. Tony Blair emphasised the priority given by Labour to achieving this target by making his first visit to a primary school within a fortnight of taking office. It was to Sudbourne Primary School in Brixton, a disadvantaged area in south London. The school had not only already reached the targets but had seen 90 per cent of its pupils reach the required standard in English and 88 per cent in maths the previous year. Mr Blair's argument was that, if this school could do it, why shouldn't others? (Incidentally, as an aside, Mr Blair's visit had to be kept secret – on security grounds – from the pupils and all at the school until the last moment. They were only told a "Very Important Person" would be arriving that day. There was speculation that it would be David Blunkett accompanied, of course, by his guide dog, Lucy. I was standing next to one father who broke the news to his son that the visitor was going to be Tony Blair, whereupon the boy started crying. "Does that mean I don't get to meet the dog?" he sniffed.)

In order to boost its chances of achieving its target, Labour was prepared to intervene where its predecessors had failed to tread and introduce a compulsory literacy hour and daily maths lesson in primary school. The way teachers should approach the literacy hour was prescriptive: they should broach what they were about to tackle in the lesson to begin with, then carry out that day's teaching and leave time at the end for recapping on what the pupils should have learned. The scheme enjoyed an instant success – by December 2000, the results of tests taken earlier in the year showed an 11 per cent rise in those reaching the required standard in English to 75 per cent, a 13 per cent rise to 72 per cent in maths and a 16 per cent rise in science (a test also taken by 11-year-olds) to 85 per cent. Michael Barber, the former NUT head of education who was now heading a school standards task force set up by the government, whilst ecstatic about the initial results, urged caution for the future, though. It would, he argued, become more difficult to secure improvements the further up the ladder you climbed. For the moment, though, it was a success story.

The new government's next action took the education world by surprise as it "named and shamed" 18 schools which had been declared "inadequate" by Ofsted two years previously and had failed to improve. The list included a range of primary, secondary and special schools and, Labour was quick to point out, included schools which had been allowed to opt out and obtain grant-maintained status under the previous Conservative administration. Mr Blunkett's number two, Stephen Byers, who had been give the title Minister for School Standards to emphasise Labour's relentless drive to see schools improve, indicated that the heads of all 18 of the schools were likely to face the sack. However, he added that the schools themselves would be given every help his department could muster in order to improve. The announcement incurred the wrath of the teachers' unions with Doug McAvoy, general secretary of the NUT, who argued "naming and shaming" was not the way forward. "Teachers at these schools are already demoralised," he added.

It was the first indication to the teachers' organisations that they would not get everything their own way and showed that the new government was going to be at least as interventionist as its predecessor in determining the way forward for the state education system. After all, the whole question of how much intervention there should be in the way state schools conducted themselves was first raised as a result of Labour Prime Minister Jim Callaghan's Ruskin College speech two decades ago when he first called for a "great debate" on education. The days of the curriculum being a "secret garden" and parents being kept in the dark about their children's school's performance were already long gone but, under Tony Blair's administration, it was obvious further strides down the road of intervention would be made.

Representatives of the teachers' organisations were to be given another example of how Labour was going to be its own boss when Mr Blunkett addressed the annual conference of the NAHT later that month and, in response to questioners, indicated that controversial chief schools inspector Chris Woodhead would keep his job as head of the education standards watchdog Ofsted. Judging by the disappointment expressed by many of the 400 heads present at the conference, you could have been forgiven for thinking that the question of whether Mr Woodhead kept his job had been a key election issue and this was Labour's first U-turn on taking office. It was not, of course. Labour had already determined he would stay in post. After all, what point would there be in a new government committed to raising standards coming in and getting rid of the man who had gained some kind of a reputation as a 'Witchfinder General' in rooting out poor standards? None, in the eyes of Labour.

So ended just a month of Labour in office.

*****

Labour did, of course, have one more thorny question to tackle upon gaining office. In the run-up to the General Election, there had been all-party agreement into setting up a committee of inquiry into university funding and student finance under the chairmanship of Sir Ron (later Lord) Dearing. One of the key outcomes of this agreement by Labour, the Lib Dems and the Conservatives had been, as indicated earlier, that the issue was not raised as a priority for debate during the election campaign. The Commission was, however, due to publish in July – just two months after Labour had taken office.

In the end, Labour accepted its recommendation that a tuition fee of £1,000 a year should be levied but the government went further than that and axed maintenance grants and introduced loans to cover the cost of student accommodation and living expenses. On the question of the fees, those whose parents were earning less than £16,000 a year were exempt from paying them and only those whose parents earned above £34,000 a year would pay the full fee. In addition, students had to be earning more than £15,000 a year before they had to start repaying their loans.

Pressure to introduce fees had come from the university vice-chancellors – particularly those in the Russell Group, which represents the most elite and hardest-to-get-into universities. There was talk that universities like Oxford and

Cambridge might consider going it alone, becoming independent and charging their own fees if the state did not introduce such a system. In the end, the £1,000-a-year fees were less than some university vice-chancellors would have liked to have seen but the package still incurred the wrath of students' leaders with Douglas Trainer, president of the National Union of Students, arguing that the new scheme would "damage access to education".

Mr Blunkett argued that it was the only way that the UK could afford a system whereby all those who could be expected to benefit from higher education could be granted access to it. (Tony Blair was later to declare that he wanted to see 50 per cent of all youngsters going on to some form of higher education.) Under the previous university funding regime, Mr Blunkett argued, it was the rich who benefitted the most from a universally free higher education system. Now all-comers would be on an equal footing and, as a result of the loans system and exemptions, no one would have to pay up-front contributions. He particularly queried why middle-class parents who had not baulked at paying out fees for independent primary and secondary should suddenly become so hot under the collar at being asked to pay for university education.

One thing the new system did, though, was to put the spotlight on efforts to persuade (and ease the path of) students from disadvantaged communities to get to university. There were fears the numbers would drop. In *The Mirror's* case, it led to us joining forces with millionaire philanthropist Sir Peter Lampl, who had set up the education charity the Sutton Trust and charged it with campaigning to secure equal access for all to education opportunities. To further this aim, he set up summer schools at four of the country's leading universities – Bristol, Cambridge, Nottingham and Oxford – aimed at the brightest pupils from disadvantaged backgrounds. The idea was that it would give them a taste of university life and erase any doubts that they might have about whether they could apply for a place at a leading university. We published a coupon in *The Mirror* for parents to send in if they believed their children warranted a place on the scheme. As a result, there were 133 applications – 17 of whom were accepted on to a summer school later that year. In the end, four succeeded in being offered places at Oxford or Cambridge – a modest number perhaps but at least these four young people were offered a place that they otherwise would not have applied for and (obviously) got. Leigh Fletcher, from Hinckley, Leicestershire, who went on to study natural sciences at Oxford's Emmanuel College, said: "I'll be the first person in my family to go to university. The summer school was wonderful." Without it, he added, he would not have thought of applying for a place at Oxford.

The campaign to persuade universities to take in more disadvantaged students reached its zenith, though, when Chancellor Gordon Brown let rip at Oxford

University for refusing a place to Laura Spence, a pupil at a comprehensive school in North Tyneside – Monkseaton High – despite the fact she was expected to get five grade As at A-level. She had wanted to study medicine and, in the end, gained a scholarship to study at the leading US university, Harvard. Soon afterwards, Oxford acknowledged that it was not taking in enough students from state schools – the figures showed that your chances of getting into Oxford were 377 to 1 if you attended a state school and only 30 to 1 if you attended a private school. As a result, it redoubled its efforts to recruit from the state sector. "I have a simple ambition: to make sure every bright teenager wherever he or she lives, whatever his or her background, thinks of applying to Oxford," said Amy Culley, schools liaison officer at Oxford University. "We are beginning to make progress. Over the last five years, the percentage of offers made to state school applicants has increased by five per cent to 53 per cent."

As for Sir Peter Lampl, he redoubled his charity's efforts in focusing on the education of disadvantaged pupils, to the extent of launching an experiment at Belvedere Girls' High School in Liverpool, a fee-paying private school. He guaranteed that no child would be turned away on economic grounds and agreed to stump up the cash for those who passed the entrance test but whose parents could not afford the fees. For years he had been campaigning for successive governments to embrace this open-access scheme – and enlisted the support of a number of private school heads for the cause, many of them former direct grant schools like Manchester Grammar. His ideal would be to turn all independent schools into open-access schools. His campaign has foundered on two grounds, though: finance – ministers believe they would be writing an open cheque as they would not know in advance how many pupils they would have to support; and selection – neither Labour nor the Conservatives have so far wanted to go back to a fully selective system of secondary schooling like that which existed at Belvedere Girls' High School.

As for the fate of disadvantaged students in higher education, the numbers admitted have flourished in latter years despite tuition fees being raised in stages to up to £9,000 a year. Official statistics from UCAS show this has not dented the numbers applying from disadvantaged groups – rather the opposite, possibly as a result of the ruling that no one has to pay a fee up-front.

*****

I was lucky enough at the end of 1997 to gain the first interview for an Education Correspondent with Tony Blair – lucky because Alastair Campbell, his head of press, had worked at *The Mirror* before joining Mr Blair's team and was sympathetic to my request.

In traditional *Mirror* style (remember the way I finally got hired by the paper!), nothing happened for a while but one day, while I was attending the conference of the Girls' Schools Association in Bristol, I had a pager message to ring the Downing Street press office. The interview was set up for the following morning and a plethora of pager messages and calls later (I was asked what I intended to ask and all sorts of things like that). As a journalist, you never want to be too forthcoming on that – mainly because it may well depend on how the interviewee answers the previous question. I was also told in no uncertain terms that if I started to pry into his private life or bring his children into the interview, it would be terminated. Imagine my surprise then when in answer to an innocuous first question: "Tell me, Prime Minister, how did you alight on the idea of having education, education and education as your first three priorities?" he answered: "Well, it's the children. They are all going through the state system. I see them in their schools and I see the benefits they get when they get a good teacher." I glanced at the press officer that had delivered me with the caution. There was no response. After all, she could hardly admonish a Prime Minister in full flight about breaching the terms of the interview.

It was an illuminating interview. He knew the issues we had been campaigning on, therefore there was a pledge of more money for school buildings. He emphasised the government's determination to bring down class sizes for five to seven-year-olds but – above all – he stuck to a theme of the "carrot and stick" approach to raising standards. Those who failed to meet targets for exam and test results would find "we are prepared to make changes in the management of the schools" (*ie* the sack). Chuffed with getting the interview, I came away from it with a copy of a photograph taken of the two of us which Anne, my wife, gave pride of place to on our stairway at home. (It disappeared on the day we invaded Iraq. Strange that. I never found it again.)

What Mr Blair did not mention, and which became the next theme New Labour adopted, was the involvement of the private sector in the running of the state sector. Professor Michael Barber, addressing the North of England Education Conference – the conference where the government set out its stall for the coming year – spoke of ministers' intentions of setting up 25 education action zones in the areas with the worst exam or test performance where firms would be given the opportunity to run up to 20 schools in the neighbourhood, have power to alter teachers' existing contracts, and pay them extra for working in the holidays to help struggling pupils catch up with their classmates. Companies that had already expressed an interest in the scheme included Tate and Lyle, the Prudential and Midland Bank. Significantly, it was welcomed by the Conservatives' then education spokesman Stephen Dorrell as "a good idea" while it was rejected almost unanimously by the teachers' organisations.

The government went on from there to initiate talks with a leading light of the Charter Schools movement in the US – Benno C. Schmidt of the Edison Project – to see if he would be interested in taking on an action zone in the UK. In the end, that did not happen although Edison did get involved in helping to run some schools in the UK. With hindsight, this flirtation with industry and the private sector can be seen as the forerunner of the academies movement – but that did not emerge until Labour's second term in office.

Labour's determination to boldly go to places previous representatives of the party had never dared to tread also manifested itself later that year when Schools Minister Estelle Morris became not only the first Labour government minister but also the first former comprehensive school teacher to address the Headmasters' and Headmistresses' Conference – the body which represents 250 of the country's most elite private schools. She promised the schools £1 million if they opened up their facilities to state schools and told the heads: "We have no wish to interfere unnecessarily with successful schools. We respect the right of parents to chose an independent school for their child."

Labour also appeared to soften its line on opposing selection after parents in Ripon had voted against scrapping the 11-plus and turning the town's grammar school into a comprehensive. "Arguments about selection are a past agenda," said Mr Blunkett. "We have set up a system which says if you don't like grammar schools you can get rid of them – but it really isn't the issue for 2000."

Pro-comprehensive campaigners complained that the rules were stacked against them – for instance, parents in any primary school which had sent a child to the grammar school were entitled to a vote (meaning the ballot was open to many parents in private schools who had no intention of sending their children to a state school while state primary schools could be disenfranchised if they had never managed to get any of their children into the grammar school).

In actual fact, Mr Blunkett's comment – though characteristically forthright – was never a departure from existing policy. Labour never meant to be sidetracked from its desire to improve standards by a succession of votes over whether grammar schools in different parts of the country should be abolished.

Incidentally, the story that I wrote for *The Mirror* which received the most adverse reaction was about grammar schools. The government had just announced that it was to declare "war" on "coasting" schools, *ie* schools that achieved respectable exam results but should be doing better because of the area they served or as a result of their selective intake. Armed with this knowledge, I looked at the exam league tables and pulled out the 10 grammar schools with the worst results – at least 10 per cent of pupils in all 10 of them were failing to get five top grade A to C grade passes at GCSE, the benchmark by which all schools were being judged. Because of their selective intake, though, they should have been closer to – if not at – 100 per cent of their intake achieving this. As John Dunford, general secretary of the Secondary Heads Association (now Association of School and College Leaders), remarked: "All 11-year-olds going to grammar schools should be expected to get five A to C passes at GCSE. The benchmark for selective schools should be very high indeed." A number of callers said I was unfairly targeting grammar schools when these schools had substantially better results than the national average. John Dunford had one angry telephone call, too, from the head of one of the 10 schools who sought to take him to task for associating himself with such a "scurrilous" article. He threatened to resign from SHA. "I wouldn't," said Mr Dunford wryly, "because I think you might be needing us soon."

Meanwhile, Mr Blunkett was in ebullient form as he became the first serving Labour Education Secretary since Shirley Williams to address the NUT conference, taking on hecklers and declaring to them: "Shouting won't make a difference. You're a tiny minority and that must be a great comfort to the 400,000 teachers who are behind our crusade." He was not given a standing ovation, but the union's general secretary Doug McAvoy was (a rare occurrence at the conference and only done to emphasise delegates' disapproval of Mr Blunkett!) when he criticised Labour's decision to "name and shame" the schools that had been on Ofsted's hit list of failing schools the longest.

Mr Blunkett attracted criticism from an unexpected quarter later on in Nobby Stiles, a member of England's World Cup winning football team of 1966. After advisers told schools they could cut down on outdoor and adventure activities to make way for spending more time on teaching the three Rs, the Manchester United footballer said: "This is absolutely stupid. Team sports are goods for developing discipline and introducing children to different games." He was not alone in expressing reservations about the lack of prominence given to school sport – Olympic champion Sally Gunnell joined in the protest, too – but the government was adamant that priority had to be give to three Rs and its crusade to improve literacy and numeracy standards.

However, all the while the government was breaking new ground in its talks with private industry and independent school representatives, it was ploughing more money into state education, it was encouraging the best performing schools to help their less well-off neighbours and it had more of an open door policy with the teachers' organisations than its predecessor, which ultimately was to lead to the setting-up of a formal discussion forum on new government policy. In other words, it was doing enough to keep the unions representing heads and classroom teachers on board and believing they had a government they could do business with.

*****

There was, however, one controversy that no one could have foreseen. It came when chief schools inspector Chris Woodhead was unwittingly taped while addressing a meeting of student teachers. During the course of a question and answer session, he told them that he believed teachers should not automatically be sacked if they had a sexual relationship with one of their pupils. Such a relationship could be "experiential" and "educative", he went on. The covert tape-recording found its way to the offices of *The Independent* and my predecessor Judith Judd. Needless to say it was a front page story and Mr Woodhead faced calls to resign – especially after it had been revealed that he had a nine-year relationship with a pupil of his at Gordano school in Bristol where he was a teacher. Mr Woodhead always insisted that the relationship did not start until after he had left the school. However, while we education correspondents were gathered at the NUT conference at Easter in 1999, we were told to expect startling developments. In fact, it was an interview with actor Tony Robinson ('Baldrick' in the *Blackadder* TV series), who had remained a close friend of Mr Woodhead's first wife, Cathy, saying the relationship had started whilst they were still at the school.

The original story broke on the Saturday morning and, by midday Sunday, Tony Blair and David Blunkett had agreed to give Mr Woodhead one last chance and allow him to keep his job. I talked to a few people who had been in touch with Mr Blunkett since the story broke and was told that he was "incandescent with rage" at what Mr Woodhead had said. It was not the official line – which was that the chief schools inspector would keep his job if he apologised for the comment – but I was confident enough that it was the truth. I remember having a conversation with Conor Ryan, Mr Blunkett's special adviser for the media, who would obviously have been very keen to find out where the information had come from. He was too professional to ask me outright – a journalist never reveals his sources – but as he said: "I can normally tell where a story has come from – but this one I can't." He never accused me of getting it wrong, though.

Mr Woodhead, therefore, survived the controversy – and the 'Baldrick' revelations. He also survived another claim by former pupils at Gordano that he had "frolicked in his underpants" with them whilst on a school trip. Mr Blunkett said of the saga: "What we have had so far is speculation and quite a lot of tittle-tattle." However, the NAHT took the matter seriously enough to ask the Director of Public Prosecutions to investigate whether he had lied about the timing of his relationship with the former pupil. As for Mr Woodhead himself, he kept silent on the affair until he was asked to address a private school conference in York just after Easter when he said: "As far as I am concerned, it is business as usual. I shall continue to run Ofsted and support Education Secretary David Blunkett in his crusade to raise standards." He survived for another 18 months as chief schools inspector – projecting the same image as he had done when he started the job. Indeed, just a day before he finally resigned from the post, he was telling MPs on the Commons education select committee that exams would have to be made harder because of the glut of pupils obtaining top grade passes. In the end, his resignation was over an offer to become a writer for the *Daily Telegraph* (he had thought initially that he could do the two jobs but Mr Blunkett insisted he would not be a party to such an arrangement). Mr Woodhead said afterwards he had decided to take up the *Telegraph* offer in order to become freer to speak out against government policy. However, not many people had noticed his reticence in speaking out whilst he had held the post. As in the case of Eric Bolton, it led to feverish speculation along the lines of "what on earth's he going to say now?"

He was replaced by Mike (now Sir Mike) Tomlinson, his deputy who had taken charge of the emergency inspection of the Ridings School in Halifax under the previous Conservative administration. He was adamant that he would maintain the Ofsted tradition of speaking up about any shortcomings he found in the system, although he did say in his interview on taking office: "I am not Chris Woodhead. That's not meant to be critical of him. But we are two very different people and it will become obvious that I have a very different way of doing things." The teaching profession breathed a sigh of relief.

*****

And so my time with *The Mirror* came to an end. I had spent 11 years there and, although it sometimes resembled a bit of a roller-coaster, it gave me some of the most fulfilling moments in my career as an education journalist. In particular, I recall the revelation about 300 teachers in Tower Hamlets praised by Ofsted facing the sack because of a government decision to axe grants which paid their salaries as teachers of English as a second language. *The Mirror's* campaigning zeal was its best feature and the other highlight of my career there was the attempt to improve the provision of nursery education. I am sure it was the focus on that which gave us the exclusive on the publication of the National Commission on Education report, headed by former government statistician Sir Claus Moser, which recommended that all three-year-olds should be entitled to a nursery place and that this provision should be phased in over a number of years, concentrating on provision for the disadvantaged. I remember then Education Secretary John Patten being asked to comment on it on the BBC Radio Four Today programme and he could not get over his astonishment that the exclusive had appeared in *The Mirror*.

Of course, it was a roller-coaster with more ups and downs than any previous or subsequent posts have had. I remember a couple of times when I was on the verge of leaving. A contact had told me about a school which was putting its pupils on a four-day week because of cuts to its education budget. It would have been the first in the country to adopt such a strategy but my news editor felt it was just a case of the headteacher "macro w***ing" and that he didn't really need to do it. Subsequently, as he was getting nowhere with me, the contact gave it to the *Today* newspaper which set off all sorts of alarm bells – and I was accused of selling the story to a rival newspaper (a heinous crime punishable by the sack). I hadn't but my protestations were considered by my news editor to be less convincing when later that day Mary Riddell, deputy editor of *Today*, rang me to offer me a job on the paper. She had previously been with *The Mirror* and had masterminded our campaign to save nursery schools from closure as editor of *Mirror Woman*. My stock being low with the news editor, I accepted the *Today* job – despite him aggressively trying to get me to promise to think again about it.

Anyhow, subsequently he left and Eugene Duffy, with whom I had worked for years on *The Mirror*, took over. A few weeks later I received a pager message from him which said: "Read page two of the *Standard* and call me." The lead story was saying that *Today* was about to close. I shall always be eternally grateful for that message. It saved my career from being nipped in the bud.

The second time I was on the verge of leaving came when the *Daily Express* offered me a job. Rosie Boycott had just taken over as editor and the idea was to relaunch as a left-of-centre tabloid. I was offered a substantial rise in salary to take the job as Education Correspondent. On this occasion, I hadn't fallen out with anybody at *The Mirror* or felt that my work was being neglected but it was just too good an offer to turn down. I went to see Piers Morgan, who had by then become editor of *The Mirror*, and we had a bizarre conversation which went something like this. "Whatever they're offering, I'll offer you £2,000 more." "But Piers you don't know what they're offering." (Negotiating for myself was never a strong point.) "Well, tell me." I did and he was as good as his word. In fact, he was better than his word. That weekend, we faced new management coming in at *The Mirror* and somehow my new salary went through the accounts machine before they arrived – otherwise I could have lost it.

One of the most touching moments following my decision to leave *The Mirror* came when I was enjoying a relaxing break watching cricket in Sri Lanka before taking up my post with *The Independent*. I knew that Matthew Lumby, who worked in the Department for Education's press team, was holidaying there at the same time and had arranged to meet him at a bar in Kandy during the lunch interval of the Test match. He handed me a letter. It was from David Blunkett: "Congratulations on your new job with *The Independent*," it said. "I am very pleased for you. God knows what will happen to coverage when you leave your present post but if anyone deserves to get the job of their choice, you do."

My frustrations at *The Mirror* had not gone unnoticed but it was not without one or two regrets that I left the paper to work for *The Independent*.

*****

And so to the 2001 election. Education did not feature as much as it had done in the 1997 campaign. You can't beat "education, education, education" as a slogan and – to a certain extent – Labour was focusing on more of the same as its election strategy. True, it did promise to take on 10,000 more teachers in its manifesto. Controversially, it ruled out university "top-up" fees for the lifetime of the next Parliament only to bring them in after they had won a third election victory in 2005. The target of 50 per cent of young people going on into higher education was set in stone. It also promised growth in the number of classroom assistants employed – to take some of the menial and administrative tasks away from teachers and allow them to concentrate more on lesson preparation. There was more emphasis on the role for the private sector in schools allowing voluntary organisations and private companies to take over the running of failing schools. They would be given a five or seven-year contract to turn the school around.

As for the Conservatives, its manifesto was interesting because it contained the first mention of its "free schools" policy. Under it, all heads would be free to make their sole criteria for admission the willingness of a parent to sign a home-school agreement. It wasn't, I believed, very well thought out. If schools had the right to exclude any pupil they did not want, how would that square with the local education authority's duty to educate every child in their neighbourhood?

At any rate, we never found out how it would work because Labour won a second substantial victory at the polls. Its time, though, would come again – and in a different form.

TIMELINE

1997

Labour introduces legislation to ban class sizes of more than 30 for five to seven-year-olds – and abolishes the Assisted Places Scheme.

Government introduces "naming and shaming" policy for schools which have been on inspectors' list of those ranked "inadequate" for the longest.

Government gives backing for tuition fees of £1,000 a year.

1998

Businesses invited to run education action zones for the poorest performing schools.

Homework charter unveiled, under which five-year-olds will study for 20 minutes in the evening.

Government pledges a nursery place for every three-year-old.

Estelle Morris become first Labour minister to address the Headmasters' and Headmistresses' Conference.

1999

Sir Peter Lampl launches summer schools to persuade disadvantaged youngsters to apply for places at top universities like Oxford and Cambridge.

Soaps *Brookside*, *Coronation Street* and *Eastenders* get called in to help the Government's crusade to improve literacy by featuring stories of adults who cannot read.

2000

Chris Woodhead resigns as chief schools inspector to take job working for *The Daily Telegraph*.

Tests for 11-year-olds show big rise in percentage of pupils reaching required standard in English (up 11 percentage points to 75 per cent), maths (up 13 per cent to 72 per cent) and science (up 16 per cent to 85 per cent.) It follows the introduction of literacy hour and daily maths lesson in primary schools.

Chapter Six
"I was Charming.
He was Offensive"

With Labour's General Election victory of 2001, David Blunkett was moved on from Education Secretary to become Home Secretary (a reward for making a success of his job in the first Blair government). I heard that when he arrived at the Home Office he called his senior press aide in and said it was his ambition to be on the front page of a Sunday newspaper every week. "Don't worry, you will, sir," came the reply – the implication being it would not always be the subject of his own choosing. That said, an assessment of his period at education would have to conclude it had been one of the more successful reigns of an Education Secretary. He had fulfilled his election pledge of reducing class sizes for five to seven-year-olds with legislation within a few weeks of taking office. His literacy and daily maths lessons for primary schools had seen a government preside over a period of improvement in reading standards for the first time since the Second World War, according to an impeccable source – the National Foundation for Education Research. Even if it did not mean that the government would hit its target of 80 per cent reaching the required standard for 11-year-olds and 75 per cent reaching it in maths by 2002 (the figures for 2001 were 75 per cent for English and 71 per cent for maths), it was still a substantial achievement. Mr Blunkett had been a forthright voice in the world of education, setting minimum times for homework for each year group and introducing vocational GCSEs in an attempt to put vocational education on an equal footing with academic education in public perception.

What of Estelle Morris, then? Well, she had street credibility, having been both taught in a comprehensive school and a teacher in a comprehensive school before she entered politics. The theme of the second Labour term was to place the emphasis on improving secondary school standards, which, roughly translated, meant an increase in private involvement in the running of education and opening academies in disadvantaged inner city areas, which would be privately sponsored – initially by paying £2 million towards the upkeep of the school. (As time wore on, this was watered down to sponsorship in kind, ie by providing facilities, and ultimately waived altogether to ensure the necessary number of sponsors came forward to meet government expectations of the policy.) During her term in office, a priority was also given to moving towards getting everyone to stay on in some form of education or training until they reached the age of 18. When she started in office, she was described as a pragmatist by her former tutor at Warwick University, Professor Jim Campbell, a follower of the "what works" tradition rather than trapped in an ideology. He said he felt she was "a kind of Blairite before Blairism was invented". Whether she would thank him for that assessment, I am not quite sure. There was also a question mark over her ability to tackle issues in higher education – she had been minister for (primary and secondary) schools in the previous government. There may have been a touch of snobbery in this assessment, a feeling that because she failed her A-levels – which she did – she was not really equipped to deal with higher education. "Not one of us", you could hear the cries from the sherry-ridden offices of some vice-chancellors.

What derailed her was the hardy old perennial of "events, dear boy", as Harold Macmillan once said. Her period in office was dogged by more controversies than she would have expected – the first of which was over a decision announced early in 2002 that she planned to scrap compulsory lessons in modern languages for 14 to 16-year-olds.

To say the decision sparked controversy was an understatement. It also paved the way for one of the most extraordinary exclusives that came my way during my 36 years as an education correspondent. The day after I had written the story I picked up the telephone in the office to find the press attaché at the German Embassy on the line to say that the German ambassador, Hans-Friedrich von Ploetz, would like a word with me about the proposal. An appointment time for an interview was fixed for two days hence and, in the intervening period, I had two further communications from the press attaché, asking whether I would mind if the Spanish and Italian ambassadors joined us for the meeting. When I arrived at the embassy, I was told that the French ambassador offered his apologies – he could not join us because of a prior engagement but he backed the sentiments that were about to be expressed by the trio at the meeting. The upshot was that they warned of what they believed was a "sad situation" evolving around the teaching of languages in UK schools. They warned that 1 in 10 British businesses were losing contracts because of their employees' inability to speak foreign languages and added that they believed the subject should be compulsory from primary school to degree level. They were also worried that the number of exchange trips between their schools and schools in the UK would fall as the number of secondary schools where pupils pursued languages until 16 would plummet. They emphasised that it was unusual for ambassadors to speak out on an issue concerning their host country's policies but that they felt it was their duty to get their message across. They had come across an open door, as far as I was concerned. I had always regretted giving up languages at A-level, believing it to be important to learn about the language and cultures of other countries. One incident that stands out in my mind as regards languages came when I heard about a holiday my brother and some friends had made to Germany. Graham, my brother, knew a smattering of German but one of his travelling companions who was having difficulty in an argument with a car-park attendant in Germany did not. He came over to him and said: "I say, Graham, can you come over and help – this peasant doesn't speak English." I thought that spoke volumes for the attitude adopted by too many Brits abroad: that they expected everyone to be able to speak their language (and, if there were any difficulties, would just speak in their own language louder than before). Imagine if you had been a German tourist in the UK: would you have expected a traffic warden to have spoken German?

Unfortunately, the reaction to the government's announcement was not sufficient for them to withdraw the proposition. It did, however, ultimately lead to ministers insisting firstly that every child should have the right to learn a foreign language from the age of seven and to making the subject compulsory in primary schools from that age – the idea being that if you introduce a language at that age to children, they will be able to pick it up more easily and therefore there would be a better chance of them continuing with it until 16. That is as maybe but it would have been an idea to have introduced that element either at the same time or before scrapping the compulsory element beyond the age of 14. The result of the policy was a massive fall in the number of pupils taking languages at GCSE level (and later A-level) by more than half (and only a partial revival came with the introduction of Michael Gove's English Baccalaureate, which insisted that schools should be measured in exam league tables on the number of pupils getting A* to C grades in GCSEs in five core academic subjects: English, maths, the sciences, a language and a humanities subject –

either history or geography. However, even that rise tailed off last year). Luckily, there are enough heart-warming tales about to restore one's confidence in the desire amongst some schools to promote the teaching of languages. Take, for instance, the case of Newbury Park primary school in Redbridge, north-east London, where the school insists every pupil should learn a smattering of all the 40 different languages spoken at the school by its children. Sadly, though, there are not enough of such tales.

The second controversy to hit Estelle Morris's reign was over the A-level results of 2002. This was the first year students were taking the new Curriculum 2000 A-levels which had ushered in the new AS-level – worth half an A-level and generally taken by pupils at the end of the first year of the sixth-form. It was, in effect, used by pupils to follow a broader range of studies in the sixth-form (usually taking four subjects in the first year and ditching the one they did worst in when it came to the full A-level). It allowed pupils to bank up marks for their grades during coursework. As a result, it became clear there was likely to be a major rise in the pass rate which Sir William Stubbs, then both chairman and chief executive of the Qualifications and Curriculum Authority, told exam boards would almost certainly mean an inquiry into the results if sustained. Some exam boards, notably the OCR, took this to mean that they should increase grade boundaries, to avoid accusations that the exam had become easier and year on year standards had not been maintained. With complaints, most vociferously made by the country's leading independent schools, into why pupils expected to get higher grades had not achieved them, an inquiry was indeed set up under the chairmanship of Mike Tomlinson, the former chief schools inspector. It concluded that exam boards had felt under pressure (as a result of Sir William's comments) to mark down papers and claimed that the crisis over marking had been "an accident waiting to happen" due to ministerial determination to rush through the reforms. In addition, there was a furious row between Ms Morris and Sir William after he accused her of interfering with the independence of the exam boards by approaching them before the inquiry to ask them how they had reached their grade boundaries – a claim she utterly denied. The upshot was, though, that on the day Mr Tomlinson published his report, she said she had decided to remove Sir William from his office. On hearing of her intention, he resigned. I had been given a leak by sources the previous day of Estelle Morris' intention – and *The Independent* ran a front page story on it. Sir William later complained that Ms Morris's advisers leaked the story with threats that those that received the briefing, *ie* me, would get no further help from them if they did not run the story in the way the advisers wanted them to. We were, according to him, bullied. Not true: the information from the sources that the man in charge of overseeing the exams was to lose his job was sufficiently newsworthy in its own right for me (or anyone else for that matter, I should think) to run it – I did not need bullying to do so. I must confess, though, to having an anxious moment when Mr Tomlinson's press conference to launch the report made no mention of Sir William's demise. I became even more anxious when I rang in to our newsdesk and heard that the editor, Simon Kelner, who was watching TV recordings of Mr Tomlinson's press conference, said he "would have my guts for garters" if the story proved untrue. Luckily, it was substantiated at a later press briefing from Estelle Morris. Although Sir William had been made the fall guy for what happened (he subsequently won compensation and a glowing tribute from Ms Morris's successor Charles Clarke after threatening to take the government to an industrial tribunal), the upshot of all this was that Ms Morris came under pressure to resign too, because of the criticism of the government's role in the saga. It had, said Mr Tomlinson, rushed through the reforms too quickly.

Around the time this was going on, another controversy emerged when it was revealed that the government had failed to meet its targets for the National Curriculum tests for 11-year-olds – 80 per cent to reach the required standard in English and 75 per cent in maths by 2002. The Conservatives unearthed a Parliamentary answer Ms Morris had given in 1999 when asked whether she would resign (as education minister) if they were not met and replied: "Of course I will." Subsequently, she told a Commons select committee in 2001 when she was asked the same question: "No, and I never said I would."

In addition, the next item on the government's education agenda was the proposal to introduce top-up fees for students at university – a policy she was not so comfortable with and in an area where she lacked expertise: higher education.

The truth is that it was probably the culmination of all these events coming together that prompted her, in an assessment confided to others, to admit that she was not "up to the job". Journalists were also said at the time to be digging into her private life and she confessed to disliking the constant scrutiny from media attention. In her first comments following her abdication when she made an unexpected appearance at a teachers' awards ceremony, she said: "This is the nicest evening I've had for six weeks". She added: "Maybe tomorrow I won't wake up at 4am."

She told teachers at the awards dinner: "You don't have to understand what I've done. You do have to understand it's not because of you. It's not that I don't still love you and believe in you."

In truth, in assessing that she was "not up to the job", she came to a conclusion that might have benefitted some of her predecessors and successors but they shirked it. She left having retained the affection of the teaching profession.

*****

Enter, then, Charles Clarke – a minister with the reputation of being more of a bruiser than his predecessor. One of his earliest tasks was to prepare MPs for the introduction of top-up fees. The Labour Party's election manifesto in 2001 had promised there would be no introduction of top-up fees in the lifetime of the next Parliament. What it had neglected to spell out was that this would mean that top-up fees would be introduced after the next Parliament – and therefore legislation to allow the government to introduce them would be put before the 2001-2005 session. It was, of course, difficult to persuade many Labour MPs, who had campaigned on the back of the election promise that there would be no introduction of new fees, to support the legislation and vote for fee rises. As Alan Johnson, who became Higher Education Minister under Mr Clarke, put it: "We decided to launch a charm offensive." Then he added: "I was charming and Charles was offensive." It was a comment that seemed to pander to the image of Mr Clarke as a tough bruiser while bolstering the reputation of Mr Johnson as somewhat more easy-going. In the end, the approach worked – but it was probably not as simple as Mr Johnson's comments might suggest. Mr Clarke had to put in a great deal of intellectually persuasive effort to convince some of the doubters in his party that they should support going down this route. Sheer offensiveness probably would not have worked (although he did say at one time when questioned about his reputation that perhaps he should show a bit more of his feminine side!).

The university vice-chancellors, in reaction to the proposal, wanted to press for fees of £5,000 a year, but that proved too much for the government to stomach. In a White Paper published in January 2003, it set out its plans for fees of £3,000 a year, the blow to be softened for the poorest students by the reintroduction of maintenance grants of £1,000 a year for those whose parents earned less than £10,000 a year. In presenting the proposals, Mr Clarke fought off an attempt by then Chancellor Gordon Brown to substitute a graduate tax for his top-up fees proposals. Mr Clarke undertook to "hit the road" and visit every corner of the country to try and convince students and academics to support the proposals. "He is not a bruiser – that's a myth," said one teachers' leader. "He listens, appraises and then states his position. He doesn't lose his temper or bully." However, the size of the problem facing him as he set out to win over the doubters came in a Commons motion signed by 50 backbench Labour MPs demanding that prestigious universities should not be allowed to charge top-up fees. At the time, it was believed that only some of the most sought-after and elite universities would charge the fees. However, it soon became clear after the White Paper that almost every university in the land would charge the maximum £3,000.

Meanwhile, during the summer months, Mr Clarke ratcheted up the pressure on backbench MPs by warning them of the dire financial consequences for higher education if universities could not receive money from top-up fees. Sweeteners were also the order of the day with Mr Clarke, as Labour Party conference time approached, floating the idea of students from poorer homes being exempt from the fees.

Ivor Crewe, president of Universities UK and vice-chancellor of Essex University, tried to put the issue in more perspective by claiming in an interview that it would cost the average student just the price of two pints a week to repay the loans for their top-up fees: "A graduate who starts off at £18,000 a year in London will be paying back £5.30p a week – which is a couple of pints of beer." He was accused by student leaders of "trivialising" the position.

Top-up fees, though, were not the only item on the agenda of higher education. Professor Steven Schwartz, vice-chancellor of Brunel University, had been charged with heading a task force to recommend a fairer admissions system for universities. Among the recommendations it came up with was the controversial proposal that would-be students from poorly performing schools – which would serve mainly disadvantaged areas – should be offered places on lower A-level grades than those from top-performing schools in the leafy suburbs. Professor Schwartz's team also backed the idea of what is known in higher education circles as PQA – post qualification application – *ie* that students should apply for their places after they get their A-level grades rather than be offered them on the back of highly dubious predicted grades from their schools. The team felt that independent schools were more likely to inflate their pupils' grades, while those from disadvantaged backgrounds would be more confident in applying for some of the country's more elite universities if they knew what grades they had achieved. The proposal had widespread backing, from Charles Clarke downwards, but due to the intransigence of the exam boards and universities in being prepared to re-arrange their schedules to allow such an arrangement it has never been implemented.

Meanwhile, support for the government's top-up fees proposal grew. Speaking for the first time about the proposals, Lord Dearing, the government fixer supremo of yesteryear and the man who drew up the report in 1997 that first suggested students should be charged £1,000 a year, backed the fees. However, he said they should be supplemented by increases in maintenance grants. He said that he would only support Mr Clarke's proposal if the ceiling on the return of grants was increased from the £1,000 suggested by the Education Secretary – a concession readily made by the government in the run-up to the crucial debate.

With decision day in the Commons looming, speculation over the fate of the proposals reached fever pitch. Even on the day of the debate it was being forecast they would be defeated by as many as 20 votes. However, one of the leading Labour rebels, Nick Brown, had been persuaded by his namesake Gordon Brown to back the proposals – being convinced that the concessions made by the government to help the poorest students were enough. In the end, the plan passed through the Commons by 316 votes to 311, with 70 Labour MPs rebelling against the government. Despite worries about a major fall-off in the number of students applying to universities, an initial drop in recruits (largely as a result of people foregoing gap years to get into universities the year before they were introduced) proved to be only temporary. Little did anyone know that in six years' time MPs would be debating raising the cap on fees to £9,000 a year.

*****

Top-up fees may have been the most controversial education proposal of the time but it was by no means the only policy being pushed through under Charles Clarke's stewardship of education.

He had a strong team under him at the department with David Miliband as his junior in the post of Schools Minister – a survivor from the Estelle Morris period of government. While Mr Clarke's eye was on the top-up fees proposal, Mr Miliband took responsibility for the launch of Labour's academies programme. With the Conservatives being wedded to a major expansion of the programme since regaining office, it can sometimes be forgotten that it was Labour that launched the idea. Initially under Labour, though, the programme was confined to trying to improve failing inner city schools – and setting up new privately sponsored academies in similar areas. The architect of the scheme, Lord (Andrew) Adonis, who was Tony Blair's chief education adviser and later went on to become Schools Minister in succession to David Miliband, was a passionate champion of getting independent schools involved in the project and sponsoring state schools. He persuaded some – most notably Wellington College and Dulwich College – through his tireless efforts but many remained resistant to the idea, arguing that if they wanted to aid state schools they would prefer to aid all the state schools in their area (by giving them access to playing fields, sharing teachers of minority subjects such as Latin and Greek and the like) and not just sponsor one. Lord Adonis, though, was convinced that, as he put it, adding the DNA of successful independent schools to state schools would be a useful ingredient in improving standards in the state sector. Arguably, there was not much difference between that philosophy and the right's determination – shown briefly in the David Cameron government of 2015 – that all state schools should become academies, *ie* run along the lines of independent schools. However, in the long term, the exam results from Labour's sponsored inner city academies showed a greater improvement than those that came in under the expanded programme started by the Coalition government in 2010. (Interestingly enough, at this time, the Conservatives shadow education spokesman Damian Green said his party would seek to bring back the policy of allowing schools to opt out of local authority – in essence also freeing them up to operate along the lines of the independent sector.)

Mr Clarke had arrived at Sanctuary Buildings – the headquarters of the Department for Education and Skills – to find a department in turmoil after the fiasco over A-level marking in 2002. His solution to that was to set up an inquiry into exam reform under Mike Tomlinson. Of that, more anon, but at least at the start it showed he was bold in tackling the problems he faced. Soon after his arrival, though, another unexpected crisis loomed on the horizon over school budgets, which meant as many as 30,000 teaching posts could be lost. At first he queried the teachers' unions' claims but then it transpired he was badly let down by civil servants about the financial situation – they had not factored in a concurrent rise in National Insurance contributions and a change in the local funding formula which meant that some schools would be badly affected. At the beginning of the 2003/04 academic year he apologised for "mistakes" in the school budget in an online missive to headteachers and stumped up extra cash. During this time, he also presided over a workload agreement – first mooted under David Blunkett's stewardship – which relieved teachers from carrying out a bevy of administrative tasks and set limits on the amount of time they could be asked to cover for absent colleagues. It was signed by everybody except the National Union of Teachers – which objected to a suggestion that teachers could double up on classes with the help of classroom assistants – and was generally perceived at the chalkface to have alleviated some of the strains teachers were under. It only began to be unpicked with the advent of the Coalition government and austerity measures. (Mr Clarke's relationship with the NUT never really picked up – he also refused an invitation to address its annual conference for a few minutes at Easter, saying he would prefer to be eating fish and chips on the seafront near his Norfolk home. A pity really – I would rather have relished seeing the forthright Mr Clarke tackle the ritualistic heckling of ministers at the conference.)

However, the biggest item on the agenda on the schools front was Mike Tomlinson's report on the future of the examination system which was largely left to Mr Miliband to deal with. Mr Tomlinson's initial report, which went out to consultation, stressed that exams should be ability-related not age-related, *ie* if you were bright and could take your GCSEs early, you should be allowed to. Mr Tomlinson was anxious to obtain as much support as he could for his proposals and counted as a breakthrough the fact that representatives of the CBI signed up for the deal. The key proposal that he managed to convince them to support was the setting up of an overarching diploma covering both GCSE and A-level results and any vocational qualifications pupils had earned. Some of the nuances of the Tomlinson report were lost in the reporting of it by sections of the media – suggestions that A-levels and GCSEs were to be scrapped were not true. However, the current GCSE and A-level system was to be reformed and replaced with the overarching diploma. (You might just as well have argued that vocational qualifications were going to be scrapped – neither were going to be scrapped, they would just be recorded alongside each other in the diploma.) This meant that an employer could still see what A-level results a potential employee had obtained but alongside them would run details of any vocational qualifications he or she had got. Mr Tomlinson's proposals envisaged toughening up A-level questions to allow more differentiation at the top (with a new A* grade), thus meeting the criticism from universities who complained that so many pupils obtained top grade passes, it was difficult to differentiate between them. However, it sought to dramatically reduce external marking of exams for GCSEs on the grounds that, in future, 16 would not be a school leaving age as everyone would have to stay in some kind of education or training until 18. The upshot of all this was that Mr Miliband, who had invested a great deal of time and effort into promoting and getting support for the package, failed to convince Tony Blair to support it. I remember him telling me that the only point that the Prime Minister seemed to be interested in was the future of A-levels. Labour was facing an impending General Election and he was mesmerised by the prospect of seeing *Daily Mail* headlines claiming that the man who once proclaimed that "education, education, education" were his three main priorities was presiding over the scrapping of what traditionalists always called the "gold standard" of the education system – A-levels. Mr Blair's official comment on the day of the report, made at a CBI dinner in Birmingham, was:

"GCSEs and A-levels will stay. So will externally marked exams." Analysts could detect a rift between Mr Blair and Mr Clarke who said the report would be followed by a White Paper early in the New Year but that doing nothing was "not an option". Soon after the publication of the Tomlinson report and Mr Blair's reaction to it, Charles Clarke was reshuffled from the education portfolio. He won what was considered promotion to the Home Office, a route followed by more than one Education Secretary which ultimately did not bestow upon them as much glory as possibly they had anticipated! He was replaced by Ruth Kelly, who perhaps lacked the intellectual muscle and background in education of Charles Clarke (who was a former president of the National Union of Students, adviser to Neil Kinnock when he was Labour's education spokesman and a junior Schools Minister before taking on the mantle of Education Secretary – I should perhaps add or declare that he was also a former schoolmate of mine at Highgate School in our younger days, although whether that adds to his gravitas or not I will leave others to decide!). One of Ms Kelly's first actions after accepting the job was to publish the White Paper Mr Clarke had referred to on the day of the Tomlinson report. Not surprisingly, in view of Tony Blair's comments on that day, there was to be no replacement of the GCSE and A-level system by an overarching diploma. Instead, a new diploma would be introduced which students could take at 16 or 18, covering a range of 14 vocational options. "We cannot afford to let intellectual snobbery leave us with a second-class, second-best vocational education system," Ms Kelly said in the Commons. However, the now ennobled Sir Mike Tomlinson confessed to being "disappointed" by the government's response. It risked, he said, "emphasising the distinction between the vocational and the academic". Thus was one of the best chances of ending that divide cut off in its prime.

*****

So ended a Parliament which proved to be much more turbulent for the government's education policies than Labour's first term of office. It had seen three Education Secretaries in contrast to the rare calm of the first administration when David Blunkett remained in office for the entire five-year period. It had witnessed the resignation of one Education Secretary who thought she was not up to the job and at least four major controversies: the scrapping of compulsory language lessons for 14 to 16-year-olds; plans to introduce top-up fees for university students in the next election; a major crisis over school budgets; and the government's refusal to accept wide-ranging reforms of the examination system recommended by an inquiry it had set up. On the plus side there was the establishment of an agreed package to reduce teachers' workload and, from the government's perspective, a successful start to its academies programme. True, not as many independent schools as ministers would have liked had so far come forward to sponsor schools but at least those which had been set up were beginning to show evidence of an improvement in standards.

Compared with all of this, the election campaign – as far as education was concerned – was comparably mundane. In the run-up to it, Tony Blair launched a 'mini-manifesto' on education in which he pledged that it would remain his top priority and that he wanted parents to be able to receive for their children the kind of education they would get at a private school. Children struggling to keep up in the basics and gifted pupils would be taught in smaller sized groups so they received more individual attention, he said. However, Phil Willis, the Liberal Democrats' education spokesman, pointed out that one of the reasons parents sent their children to private schools was the smaller class sizes and reducing class sizes was one pledge the Prime Minister did not make. All in all, the 'mini-manifesto' was interpreted mainly as a growth in the academies programme if Labour were to be re-elected.

Along with the 'mini-manifesto', another 'mini-controversy' emerged over the Channel Four programme *Jamie's School Dinners*, fronted by the celebrity chef Jamie Oliver. As a result of his campaign for healthier school dinners, a total of 271,000 parents had signed a petition demanding that the government take action. Oddly, the night before Mr Oliver was due to present his petition at Downing Street, I had a telephone call from someone (who had better remain anonymous) asking if I wanted any reaction to an announcement that the government was going to make more money available to schools to improve kitchen facilities and provide pupils with healthy eating options. He hadn't got details of the amount being spent but assumed it was being leaked to the following morning's papers. It wasn't but, armed with that information, I contacted a government spokesman to find out if the story was true. At first, he was very cagey but when I suggested it wasn't that much that would be on offer (small potatoes, I suppose you could have called it), he became a bit ratty and said it was £280 million. Thank you and goodnight. I had the story. Asked the following day whether parents should be thanking her or Jamie Oliver for the improvement to school dinners, Ruth Kelly replied: "I'd like to think both." To be fair to her she had been pressing the issue before Jamie Oliver's petition. However, Phil Willis, for the Liberal Democrats, said it was "sad that it had taken a celebrity chef to get the government to act". When junior minister Stephen Twigg announced the package on the same day to the NASUWT conference, delegates laughed. They were particularly unimpressed by a suggestion education standards watchdog Ofsted should inspect school food. "Presumably what they do is simply try school meals and wait until the following morning," said Chris Keates, its general secretary.

At the time, Ms Kelly was going through a difficult time, having been described the previous weekend by Hilary Bills, the incoming NUT president, as the worst Education Secretary since Labour was re-elected in 1997 (*ie* worse than David Blunkett, Estelle Morris and Charles Clarke). Mrs Bills added: "She doesn't come over as being well-briefed. The whole way she talks to teachers is with a patronising attitude." She was particularly upset by Ms Kelly's decision to abandon the Tomlinson report proposals and her suggestion – made in her first conference speech – that schools should talk more to parents which, she said, was an example of her "patronising attitude".

Ms Kelly retained her post, though, when Labour won the General Election.

TIMELINE

2002

Ministers announce they will ditch compulsory language lessons for 14 to 16-year-olds.

Estelle Morris sets up an inquiry into A-level results which finds that exam boards believed they were under pressure from Sir William Stubbs, head of the Qualifications and Curriculum authority, to lower grade boundaries.

Government fails to meet target of 80 per cent of 11-year-olds to reach required standard in English and 75 per cent in maths.

Estelle Morris resigns after Conservatives reveal she had promised she would if the targets were not met. Charles Clarke takes over as Education Secretary.

A plan for top-up fees for university students is the most controversial proposal in Queen's Speech.

2003

First City academies – privately sponsored in inner city areas – open in September.

95

Local education authorities unanimously back the introduction of the six-term year – which will reduce summer holidays and avoid loss of learning by pupils during the long summer break.

2004

MPs vote by 316 to 311 in favour of introducing top-up fees.

Conservatives say they will bring back schools opting out of local authority control if they win the next election.

The Tomlinson report on exam reform recommends an overarching diploma to cover both A-levels and GCSEs as well as vocational qualifications. Tony Blair pours cold water on the idea.

2005

Ruth Kelly takes over as Education Secretary. Announces she will not accept Tomlinson proposal for overarching diploma and instead will set up separate diplomas to cover vocational education.

Government gives £280 million to provide healthier school dinners after Jamie Oliver's Channel Four series prompts a 271,000-signature petition from parents on the subject.

Chapter Seven
Going. Going. Gove

The government's academies agenda was top of the priority list for Labour in education after the 2005 election – and Ruth Kelly was returned to office to drive it through. In language similar to that adopted by David Cameron later after the 2015 election, Tony Blair had talked during the campaign about every school becoming self-governing. Sir Cyril Taylor, government adviser on academies and head of the Specialist Schools and Academies Trust, had also raised the thorny question of forced academisation, *ie* compelling failing schools to become academies with a new private sponsor. Mr Blair was setting the government a target of 200 privately sponsored academies being set up by the time of the next election while Sir Cyril revealed there was a hit list of 170 schools earmarked for the forced academies programme. "These schools have 150,000 children receiving a very low standard of education," he said. "Many drop out before they're 16. They don't have the skills to get jobs. Many will spend their lives on welfare or – worse – get into crime." Ruth Kelly's task was to promote the programme and try to get her party backbenchers to embrace it. She had as her Schools Minister the enthusiastic Andrew Adonis – the architect of the academies programme – but it was still proving a hard sell. The summer's exam results brought a boost of a kind to the programme with Thomas Telford school, one of the first City Technology Colleges – the forerunners of the academies programme in the Kenneth Baker era – getting the best GCSE results for the state sector and doing better than all the remaining 164 selective state grammar schools in the process. It was just one of two non-selective schools to achieve a 100 per cent record in the number of pupils gaining five A* to C grades at GCSE – the other was also a CTC: Brooke Weston in Corby,

Northamptonshire. Critics pointed out that the schools had achieved their results by putting pupils in for vocational qualifications – deemed to be worth the equivalent of four GCSE passes – but it is worth pointing out that when the system changed to rank schools on the percentage of pupils getting five A* to C grades including maths and English, Thomas Telford was still on top of the perch. The Prime Minister repeated his claim that he wanted to see every state school become a self-governing school as he published a White Paper on Labour's planned education reforms in the autumn. In the process, he courted a row with senior backbench Labour MPs and even within the Cabinet with the Deputy Prime Minister John Prescott speaking up against the proposals. He was just one of many senior Labour Party figures who voiced concern at stripping powers away from the local authorities and he expressed fears that the policy would benefit the few rather than the many. Left-wing rebel in those days but now Jeremy Corbyn's Shadow Chancellor, John McDonnell, put it more bluntly: "It's all part of the privatisation agenda. The mood in the party is that enough is enough because it will be us facing the backlash in the public reaction to these policies at the next election, not the Prime Minister." Mr Blair had promised to stand down during the lifetime of this Parliament to ease the passage of Chancellor Gordon Brown to taking on the top job. The influential Commons Select Committee on Education, under the chairmanship of long-serving Labour MP Barry Sheerman, argued that the government should await the results from the first 17 academies it had set up before rushing headlong into an expansion of the programme. Later he said of the drafting of the reform document: "It is an extraordinarily poorly written piece of work. If I was still a lecturer and you were a student, I would say there is some good stuff here – but go away and give it more shape and form." The eventual White Paper left the proverbial cigarette paper between Labour and the Conservatives on academies, calling for all schools to be given the right to opt out of council control. (Remember Labour had abolished opting out on gaining office in 1997.) It just did not go quite as far as the proposals announced in 2016 by then Chancellor George Osborne's budget, when he pledged that all schools would be forced to become academies by 2022. The new breed of schools, according to Labour, would be named 'trust' schools and could be run by private companies, voluntary organisations, faith groups or parents' co-operatives. When Ms Kelly tried to defend the policy at the first major conference of the year – the North of England Education Conference in Gateshead – she faced cries of "shame" from teachers and local authority representatives. When she insisted the schools should be at arm's length from local authorities, there were shouts of "why?"

Outside of the academies drive, the government was still facing flak for its decision to drop compulsory language lessons for 14 to 16-year-olds. In a fiery farewell speech – by ambassadorial standards – the outgoing German Ambassador to London Thomas Matussek insisted "English is not enough" for tomorrow's youngsters. He urged the government and local education authorities to ensure languages had "a firm place in school life" and regretted that the take-up of the subject was "unfortunately still falling".

Another controversy emerged after a review by Ms Kelly's officials and police showed that 88 people registered as sex offenders had not been banned from schools. She steered her way through this problem – which, to be honest, was not of her making – by announcing a thorough review of the controversial cases.

The battle, though, over 'trust' schools, academies, opted-out schools – call them what you will – continued. The government's case appeared to take a hit when one of the first academies to be established, the 1,200-pupil Unity Academy in Middlesbrough, failed its Ofsted inspection for the second time. Labour rebels were quick to point out what they saw as a flaw in the government's proposals: if it was a local authority school, the government's solution would be to force it to become an academy, but what do you do with a failing academy? The answer appeared to be that you sacked the sponsors and found another set but that was not enough to appease the programme's critics. At the same time, Ms Kelly was drafting a new code on school admissions which would prevent schools selecting pupils by stealth – one of the great fears rebel Labour MPs had over the academies programme. Under it, schools would be barred from asking parents whether they were married or what jobs they had – questions which had in the past led some schools to favour pupils from more affluent homes or families considered to be stable in their admissions processes. All this effort, though, culminated in a government reshuffle which saw Ms Kelly moved from her post. Her departure was perhaps most diplomatically dealt with by Philip Parkin, general secretary of the Professional Association of Teachers, who said: "Ruth Kelly had to endure a great deal during her time in office. Many of the issues and the circumstances she faced weren't kind to her ... I hope she has a longer and more positive time in her new post." Her replacement was Alan Johnson, the charming half of the "charm offensive" launched with Charles Clarke to persuade backbench Labour MPs to back top-up fees. It had worked that time. Now it looked as though a new "charm offensive" was necessary to push through the government's 'trust' school proposals.

*****

Within weeks of taking office, Alan Johnson found his first major task would be steering the 'trust' school proposals through the House of Commons. In the event, 46 Labour MPs did rebel against the government but the measures to set up the new breed of schools were passed with the support of Conservative MPs. Mr Johnson warned rebels afterwards that Labour would not drop its reform agenda so other controversial issues were likely to follow. In the end, it was quite comfortable for the government – just three days before the vote there had been talk of up to 70 MPs rebelling against the proposals rather than the 46 that did.

Meanwhile, the education world saw the introduction of another Johnson on to the scene – Boris, who became the Conservative Party's higher education spokesman. Speaking at the launch of a personal pamphlet outlining his thinking on higher education finance, he suggested that students who did well at A-level should receive higher grants. "What if you decided to offer an academic bonus and for every A grade you got a £1,000 grant?" he said. The idea never caught on but it was good headline material. One other thing he announced at the same launch was that the Conservatives had ditched their policy of opposing the expansion of higher education (Tony Blair had said at the previous election – and in the run-up to it – that 50 per cent of young people should go on to higher education). Mr Johnson described the Conservatives' previous policy as "a load of rubbish". "The problem was our policy was considered elitist," he said. "We were knocking on doors and saying to people that university was not for them."

Back to the government's agenda, and it appeared education had won breathing space from further controversy. However, the next Queen's Speech in November 2006 spoke of radical reforms to further education to give colleges degree awarding powers. The idea was being mooted that, with the advance of online communications, you could study for a degree at one of the country's most popular universities from your local further education college, thus removing the necessity to have to pay stiff away-from-home accommodation fees. It was already the case that the advent of top-up fees had coincided with a major increase in the number of young people (18 to 25-year-olds) studying for their degrees at the Open University. It allowed them to "earn while they learned", holding down a job whilst they studied for a degree and was considered by many to be a sign of things to come.

Tony Blair, in what was being billed as his "legacy" speech on education before departing the scene, unveiled plans for a new "supergrade" at A-level – the A* – as part of the long-term response to university admissions officers claiming it was too difficult to differentiate the high flyers from the rest now that around one in four students who took A-levels achieved an A grade. It was, some observers argued, his first sop to the Tomlinson report on A-levels. Sir Mike had argued there could be an A** and even an A*** grade to achieve the same purpose. With a growing number of independent schools seeking to put their pupils in for alternatives to A-levels, he predicted an expansion in the number of state schools offering the International Baccalaureate to their pupils. The government, he said, would provide funding for up to 100 extra state schools to offer the IB by 2010. At the time he was speaking, the number offering it was just 48. The IB offered a broader sixth-form curriculum to its students – insisting they studied seven subject areas instead of just three under the traditional A-level curriculum. At Sevenoaks School in Kent, the independent school which pioneered the move to the IB, IB students complained they were taking the harder option compared to A-level students when the school ran the two qualifications side by side. Eventually, it moved completely over to the IB.

Another strand of Tomlinson's thinking came to be adopted by the government at the same time when Alan Johnson announced proposals for fast-tracking bright pupils so they could take their national curriculum tests and exams early. The proposal had actually been given backing by an inquiry team headed by Christine Gilbert, the then Chief Inspector of Schools, the previous week in a report which warned that too many pupils were getting "stuck" in the state system and failing to make progress in the three Rs.

At the same time, Mr Johnson moved forward with the proposal – that had been floating around for some time – that all young people should stay on in education or training until they reached the age of 18. A Green Paper fleshing out the details of the proposals raised the prospect of teenagers being fined if they failed to stay on in education. There would, said Mr Johnson, be £50 fixed penalty notices with the prospect of court action if they were not paid. However, it is worth pointing out that the proposals were a far cry from raising the school leaving age to 18 as some of the more robust headlines proclaimed. You could satisfy the demands of the Green Paper by undergoing one day a week of skills training for the job you had taken up.

Two other measures emerged during the tail end of Mr Johnson's reign at the Department for Education and Skills: all-white pupil schools were to become legally obliged to twin with a multi-ethnic school in a bid to promote greater cultural awareness throughout the country; and, on languages, Lord Dearing, appointed to head an inquiry into the teaching of modern foreign languages, suggested the subject should become compulsory from the age of seven and that the decision to end compulsory lessons for 14 to 16-year-olds should be reviewed if evidence from extending the subject to primary schools failed to show any major advance in the take-up of the subject in GCSE years. At the same time, all specialist language colleges were told by government adviser Sir Cyril Taylor they should put Mandarin on the curriculum as trading with the Far East was becoming more vital to the UK economy. "It is a strategic world language," he said. "The difficulty in the past has been getting Chinese teachers. However, exchanges between our schools and Chinese schools will help to change that." His Specialist Schools and Academies Trust had clinched a deal with the Chinese government for it to send 200 teachers a year over to the UK to teach Mandarin in schools.

Summing it up, it meant that Mr Johnson's regime – after the initial controversy of steering the 'trust' schools programme through the Commons – was essentially a tidying-up process in which a number of perhaps less eye-catching but important initiatives were launched. The longest-lasting reforms were the introduction of the A* grade and further moves towards the introduction of languages into the primary school curriculum. The IB never took off to the extent that Tony Blair might have hoped, while the proposal to get all young people to remain in education or training until the age of 18, although adopted by the succeeding Coalition government and (now) the Conservatives, was never quite given the impetus it should have been. I doubt whether anyone will ever receive a fixed penalty notice of £50 for failing to register for a course or training. The trouble is, without teeth to back the proposal up, it is unlikely to be as successful at it should be.

Mr Johnson's regime ended with the arrival of Gordon Brown as Prime Minister. A government reshuffle gave the education portfolio to Ed Balls. Where did Mr Johnson end up? You've guessed it: the Home Office.

*****

At about this time, another major issue began to dominate education conference debate: the question of whether UK pupils were the most tested in the education world and what effect that was having on their schooling and their psyche.

To be honest, the debate had first surfaced a few years earlier with the introduction of national curriculum tests for 7, 11 and 14-year-olds but was gaining impetus as a result of a few "add-ons" to the testing regime.

It was a debate that hit the headlines for the first time at the National Association of Head Teachers' conference in May 2006 when heads claimed the time spent on testing was overcrowding the curriculum and thus leaving little time for creativity and enjoyment of learning. That prompted *The Independent* to ask: "Is there too much testing of children in British schools?" Pupils were becoming bored with their lessons and were switching off learning. The NAHT drew attention to the seven ages of testing: in addition to the National Curriculum tests, there were baseline assessments to test what pupils could do at the age of five, GCSEs, AS-levels taken at the end of the first year of the sixth-form and A-levels. With the advent of the Coalition government, a new test (or phonics check) was introduced at the age of six to help identify slow readers – although teachers claimed that bright children (or good readers) often failed this because they knew the words were made up (or wrong in their eyes). They sought to replace them with real words that sounded similar – and were thus marked down. Move on to the present Conservative government and plans to use tests to rank schools on the progress they had made with their pupils by comparing their results on entry in baseline assessments with those that they achieved at 11 were unveiled. In addition, there was to be a times table test in maths towards the end of primary schooling. To be fair, to ameliorate the pressures during Ed Balls's reign as Education Secretary, the tests for 14-year-olds were scrapped. The Conservatives also had to abandon their plan to use the baseline tests to rank schools when it was pointed out that they were not comparing like with like due to the number of different tests schools were using. The point was still valid, argued heads and teachers: UK pupils were still the most tested in the western world.

In that assessment, they were backed up by Dr Ken Boston, who had taken over at the Qualifications and Curriculum Authority after the demise of Sir William Stubbs. Dr Boston said he believed UK youngsters were overburdened compared with the rest of the world. Sir Mike Tomlinson, he of the report that the government did not have the courage to implement, also said he felt that today's youngsters were less capable of using their knowledge to develop an argument in an essay because they were constantly being "taught to the test". All governments, though, have claimed that the issue of testing was "non negotiable".

There the matter remained for the best part of a year until a headline-grabbing report from UNICEF claimed Britain's children were "unhappy, neglected and poorly educated". They came 20th out of 21 when ranked on happiness. UK youngsters were among the least like to enjoy school, it added. On education, the UK was ranked 17th – scoring poorly because of the lack of pupils being persuaded to stay on in education and training after the age of 16. They were also 18th when it came to measuring the amount of poverty and inequality, despite the country being the fifth largest economy in the world. One measure showed they were in the bottom third when it came to the number of books they had access to at home. In two other categories, for the stability of families and friendship and indulgence in sex, drink and drugs, they came bottom. Overall, that placed them bottom – just behind the United States. The Netherlands, Sweden and Denmark took the top three places when it came to measuring children's wellbeing. A comment passed on to Sue Palmer, child psychologist and author, probably summed up the dilemma. "While chatting with teachers in the Netherlands, I mentioned that many British children now start learning the three Rs when they've just turned four," she said. "The women teachers' faces contorted with horror. 'But that's cruel,' they said. 'They should be playing out in the sunshine.' Their headteacher burst out laughing. 'Over here on the mainland, we think you Anglo-Saxons are mad,' he said." The children themselves were given a voice in the report. "I am doing my GCSEs at the moment and there is a huge amount of pressure that I am under from my teachers and my parents to do well," said Leo, aged 14, from north London. "There is a lot of coursework to complete and I am always being nagged at to do things like homework clubs and revision tests. The other thing that annoys me about my situation is that I feel that whatever I am doing there is always somebody watching over me."

The theme was developed a year later in the widest-ever ranging inquiry into primary schooling in the UK conducted by Cambridge academic Professor Robin Alexander. Parents, he argued, were choosing schools on the basis of their league table positions and, as a result, England was unique in using testing to control what was taught in schools. Research showed there was an increase in the number of schools cheating to obtain good national curriculum test results – in the past year up to 2008, four schools had their results disqualified while 14 had some pupils' results docked. Education Otherwise, the organisation which supports parents who educate their children at home, reported a significant rise in the numbers choosing this option. Whilst the risk from drugs and a growing knife culture in some areas were cited as key reasons for deciding to educate children at home, it was also felt that some parents were unhappy with the pressures put upon their children by constant testing. The final report echoed these sentiments but was criticised by Mr Balls who said the authors were "out of touch with the concerns of parents I speak to around the country who want to know their children are learning the basics of English and maths". However, as *The Independent* observed: "This was the government that promised its priority would be education, education, education. Instead, as a slew of extraordinary reports are making clear, it will be remembered as the government that could not leave well alone."

A host of experts rallied to Professor Alexander's theme. Professor Alan Smithers, head of the Centre for Education and Employment at Buckingham

University, said: "The government might have been warned by the collapse of the Soviet economy which depended on numerical targets, strategies and sanctions. What has happened to the Soviet economy is not unlike what happened to Soviet industry." Speaking to the National Education Foundation, Estelle (now Baroness) Morris, who had normally been supportive of the government's agenda since leaving office, added: "We thrash around from one initiative to another."

While the government was dismissive of the Alexander report (and had set up its own inquiry into primary education under former leading schools inspector Jim Rose), the wider education world took up the theme again. The Association of Teachers and Lecturers called for a Royal Commission to be set up to find out why our children were so unhappy. "We believe stress and mental health would be reduced by a different approach to schooling," said Dr Mary Bousted, its general secretary. That, she argued, would recognise the fact that, in order to be successful, you had to fail sometimes along the way. She said the excessive testing regime was making pupils mentally ill. Children's authors – including Philip Pullman (author of the *His Dark Materials* trilogy), Michael Rosen (former Children's Laureate) and Jacqueline Wilson (author of the Tracey Beaker books) – also rallied to back a campaign to scrap the SATs (the national curriculum tests).

That summer produced more evidence of a testing regime in turmoil as results of the national curriculum tests taken by 1.2 million 11 and 14-year-olds were delayed after the contract to oversee the tests and deliver the results was given to a private contractor, ETS Europe, for the first time. The upshot was the second QCA chief executive in succession, Dr Ken Boston (after Sir William Stubbs), was forced to quit his £180,000-a-year job. It was understood at the time that he was given little option with a source close to Ed Balls saying the delivery of the SATs results was "not their (QCA's) finest hour". Later Mr Balls announced the ending of national tests for 14-year-olds – although schools would still be free to deliver their own tests if they felt they needed to check on pupils' progress at that age. That, though, was not enough to head off calls for a boycott of the 11-year-old SATs the following summer on the grounds they were burdensome and putting too much pressure on both teachers and pupils. The call was passed at both the NUT and NAHT conferences, making it the first issue that the new government would have to deal with in education after the 2010 election – as the tests were due to be sat within a couple of weeks of polling. "We've got to show Ed we've got Balls," said one NUT delegate during the debate. Fine – but, in the end, it wasn't Ed Balls that they had to show that to. The NAHT, by the way, was a relative stranger to industrial action but the move was passed overwhelmingly at its annual conference. The issue was, not to put too fine a point on it, one of the best examples of the clashes between a hyperactive government and a recalcitrant profession to emerge during the four decades that this book covers. It highlighted the growing divergence between professionals on the ground and politicians determined to prescribe what they should be doing.

*****

Meanwhile, the Conservatives were building up a bank of opposition policies on education on which to fight the next General Election. It all started with the advent of Michael Gove, the former *Times* journalist, to the post of Shadow Education Secretary in July 2007. As so often with significant political events, it hardly seemed to have happened as a result of forward planning. David Willetts had held the shadow education brief since the previous election and got embroiled in a row with Conservative backbenchers.

For a while now, policy in both the major political parties on selection had been stagnating. Neither were committed to ending grammar school status for the 164 remaining selective schools within the state system. Neither, either, were committed to increasing the number of grammar schools.

David Cameron, now party leader (and a former education spokesman) made it clear in a speech as early as January 2006 that there would never be a return to grammar schools under him. David Willetts, therefore, felt he was just emphasising party policy when he made a speech explaining why there would be no return to selection under the Conservatives. "Academic selection," he argued, "entrenches advancement, it does not spread it." Figures showed that the percentage of pupils on free school meals in grammar schools was about a sixth of the national average of around 15 per cent. His speech, though, sparked a major controversy with backbenchers – and one senior party spokesman, Graham Brady, who covered European issues for the Conservatives, resigned his post as a result of Mr Willetts's intervention.

Mr Brady, an MP representing the Trafford area, which retained selection, had always been a keen advocate of selection and was a leading light in the National Grammar Schools Association. He argued that obtaining a grammar school place was the best way out of a life of disadvantage for pupils from poorer homes. As a result of the furore, when it came to reshuffle of shadow posts a couple of months later, Mr Willetts was moved away from education and given a brief just to speak on higher education. Many non-Conservatives felt they had lost someone who at least empathised with what they were trying to achieve in education.

Enter, then, Michael Gove and the start of the most coherent attempt to put an education policy in place for the Conservatives since their departure from office. One of his earliest targets as an opposition spokesman was to criticise the government's new diplomas – seen by Mr Balls as the natural successor to A-levels in years to come. Mr Gove told the Commons select committee on education that the Conservatives wished to "preserve and enhance" A-levels. In particular, he would scrap three academic diplomas announced by Mr Balls – in the humanities, languages and science. He described them as "a mistake and a wrong turning". It appeared his mistrust of the diplomas programme was vindicated when David Laws, the Liberal Democrats education spokesman, unearthed figures which showed that 55 per cent of secondary schools had failed to sign up to the diplomas despite their imminent introduction into the curriculum.

His next intervention came as a result of a government reshuffle which involved "Mr Academies", Lord Adonis, being switched from his schools brief to take on a new role at transport. Mr Gove said he had been "kicked out" because he was more "gung-ho" about academies than Ed Balls. Both he and his leader David Cameron were quick to offer Lord Adonis a post in a Conservative administration if he wanted it. He would, though, have to rescind his Labour Party membership. It was a sign of the Conservatives' growing faith in the academies programme. Lord Adonis declined the offer and revealed at the same time that he had always been passionate about transport – so the switch of briefs was no demotion for him. That may have come as a surprise to some observers but the enthusiasm he then showed for his new brief made it more believable. Within weeks, too, the government announced an expansion of its academies programme as if to disprove the theory that the reshuffle had anything to do with a clash of opinions between Lord Adonis and Mr Balls. Under the expansion plan, 70 failing schools would be closed within two years and reopened as academies, run by private sponsors.

Going back to Mr Gove's programme, though, the main thrust was announced in a blueprint for the future unveiled to coincide with the Conservative Party conference. The academies programme would be expanded to allow all good and outstanding schools to convert to academy status. There would also be a network of free schools set up around the country, run by parents' groups, faith groups, voluntary organisations, teachers and private companies, to supplement the state sector and offer parents an alternative for their children. It was, he said, based on a model already operating in Sweden. I have to thank him for that as it saw me on an aeroplane as soon as possible to check out the Swedish model. I found that the Swedish system did encourage a multitude of suppliers

– Montessori, faith groups and schools which just had a traditional ethos. Michael Sandström, the Swedish Prime Minister's chief adviser on education, indicated his support for the project by telling me his daughter was attending a free school where all the pupils had to stand up when a teacher entered the room. "Not usual for Sweden," he said. The result of the programme, though, was a mixed picture: there was an increase in the segregation of pupils (along racial lines). Results showed the independent free schools doing better than the remaining municipal schools but that could have been put down to their middle class intake. One thing Mr Sandström impressed on me was his belief that Mr Gove's plan just would not work unless he allowed providers to make a profit out of running schools – there just would not be enough interest in coming forward otherwise. (Incidentally, just as an aside, I was very impressed by the openness of the Swedish government during my stay in Sweden. Before I arrived, I was told to ring up and fix an appointment with Mr Sandström when I got to Stockholm. "Oh, yes," I thought. "Very likely." Briefings in Whitehall are seldom arranged at such notice – but I had no trouble in arranging an interview.) In the years after Mr Gove announced his free school policy, though, Sweden slid down the international league tables for performance in reading, numeracy and science. As a result Mr Gove tended to emphasize in later years that his policy was based on the Charter programme in the United States – where, once again, remarkable success stories were mixed with schools that had not fared so well. Never mind the mixed results, though: the Conservatives' free schools programme was here to stay.

The rest of Mr Gove's blueprint for the election included tougher O-levels and GCSEs, a demand that all would-be primary school teachers should have at least a B grade at GCSE in maths – instead of the C grade at present – and sweeping new powers for headteachers to check on their teachers' classroom performance. A blueprint for the Conservatives devised by Sir Richard Sykes, former vice-chancellor of Imperial College London, envisaged an elimination of coursework for GCSE and A-level exams and a concentration on the final end-of-syllabus exam. This part of Sir Richard's blueprint was generally welcomed by Mr Gove (and eventually implemented when he was in power). Mr Gove did not adopt another section of the report which called for students to have to sit separate standardised tests to gain entrance to university. Sir Richard argued this would help admissions staff sort out the brightest pupils as so many were gaining top grade passes but Mr Gove argued this might not be necessary if the government had succeeded in making A-levels tougher.

All in all, the style in which Mr Gove conducted himself in opposition bore similarities to the way that David Blunkett had beavered away drawing up policy options before the 1997 election. Both had a comprehensive programme for implementing when they took office when compared to other opposition education spokespeople I had come across. Both, incidentally, were successful in that they took office after the election.

*****

Meanwhile, though, Labour was still in control of the education system. Mr Balls sought to introduce some subtle shifts in the government's academies programme by shifting the emphasis away from private companies sponsoring academies to universities. He also announced he was waiving the £2 million fee for sponsoring an academy (which, admittedly, had not been policed that heavily). It would, it was argued, open the programme up to more than just rich private sponsors. It also emerged that Mr Balls was not quite so keen on faith schools (he was sceptical of some of their admissions policies which included getting parents to pledge money before agreeing to find a child a school place) as Mr Blair. He made it clear there was no priority in his department to increase the number of faith schools. One policy that Mr Balls was keen on, though, was the diploma programme – so much so that he predicted it would become the "qualification of choice", taking over from A-levels as he sought to widen its popularity by announcing three new diplomas in core academic subjects: the humanities, languages and science. His optimism was to be rebuffed, though, when it emerged the take-up of the programme was far lower than the government had estimated. One diploma, however, that in engineering, was considered to be top class and was granted recognition by Cambridge University, which saw it as the best indication as to whether a teenager was gifted in education that the system had ever had. But in the long term, its popularity proved not to be enough to sustain the programme.

Otherwise, Mr Balls's reign was dominated by a series of bread-and-butter issues – he presided over the publication of a report by the government's "behaviour tsar", Sir Alan Steer, on discipline in schools which came to the common sense solution that if teaching standards improved, so would behaviour as pupils became more interested in their lessons. In an interview I did with him after the publication of the report he urged schools which frequently suspended pupils for two or three weeks at a time to think again as to whether their policy was successful. "Sending them to the head and giving them a right royal rollicking could be better than giving them a fixed-term exclusion," he said. "Some schools seem to have very high levels of fixed-term exclusions. I don't see that as showing you're tough on discipline ... You might need to rethink your strategy if a pupil is excluded again and again. They just get used to being out of school." He also called for it to be enshrined in law that a teacher could use powers such as detention and confiscation to impose order because too many parents were challenging schools' discipline problems in the courts.

Other examples of the Balls regime in action included a plan to introduce MOT-style tests for teachers – checking on their standards after five years in the classroom. He was also a massive supporter of trying to promote the teaching of Mandarin in schools as he believed the UK's trading future lay in achieving more trade with China. He wanted a school in every town to be teaching the subject.

In a sense, though, the Balls regime could be regarded with hindsight as almost the calm before the storm for an education system which was about to be hit by sweeping new changes with the advent of a Coalition government with Michael Gove at the helm of the education system.

On the higher education front, meanwhile, the country found itself in a similar position to that in 1997 when all three main political parties had agreed to the setting up of an inquiry by Lord Dearing into the funding of higher education to take the issue of student fees off the agenda. This time it was Lord Browne who had been asked to conduct a review. It didn't quite take the heat out of the debate because the Liberal Democrats campaigned hard against the introduction of fees with, as we shall see, disastrous consequences for their future. It did mean, though, that any major decisions were put off until after polling day.

TIMELINE

2006

Conservative Party leader David Cameron declares he will not seek a return to grammar schools.

Ruth Kelly says all new schools should be "at arm's length" from local education authorities.

Student numbers drop as top-up fees regime of up to £3,000 a year comes in.

2007

Alan Johnson replaces Ruth Kelly as Education Secretary.

UNICEF report says Britain is the worst place in the world to grow up.

David Willetts is reshuffled from shadow education after explaining why the Conservatives do not want a return to grammar schools. Michael Gove takes over as the Conservatives' education spokesman.

Student numbers start to go up again.

2008

Biggest ever inquiry into primary education is heavily critical of testing regime.

Ken Boston quits as chief executive of the Qualifications and Curriculum Authority as a result of a summer fiasco in which national curriculum test results were delivered late to 11 and 14-year-olds and their schools by the private company brought in to oversee them.

Michael Gove outlines his plans for a new breed of free schools.

2009

Both NUT and NAHT back a boycott of national curriculum tests for 11-year-olds after claiming they put too much pressure on both teachers and pupils.

Teachers' right to use detention and confiscation should be enshrined in law to protect schools from over-litigious parents, says government's behaviour tsar Sir Alan Steer.

2010

Ed Balls calls for an expansion of Mandarin teaching in schools.

General Election ushers in a new Coalition government with Michael Gove at the helm of education.

Chapter Eight
And now for something completely different ... Education, education, education

Michael Gove swept into Sanctuary Buildings – the home of the Department for Education – in May 2010 just as enthusiastically as New Labour under David Blunkett had done in 1997. He had promised during the election campaign to give a "rocket boost" to the academies programme – and within a couple of weeks of taking office was paving the way for all schools rated as "outstanding" in inspections by Ofsted to have the automatic right to claim academy status from September, *ie* just four months from the accession of the new Coalition government. Figures showed this would open the door to up to 600 secondary schools and, for the first time, up to 2,000 primary schools. In the end, the initiative started with more than a whimper than a roar with only 32 schools able to open as new academies at the start of the academic year in September. However, the numbers gradually grew to the extent that eventually more than half the secondary schools in the country became academies, and while take-off was a little more limited in primary schools, thousands did still sign up. Mr Gove also pushed ahead with his plans to open up 'free' schools giving parents, teachers, charities and private companies the right to set up their own schools

– the first of which were to open in September 2011. Early indications showed around 700 expressions of interest in the idea. One of the Liberal Democrats' most cherished policies – the pupil premium (which, incidentally, was supported in varying forms by Labour and the Conservatives during the election campaign) – also featured in the first Queen's Speech of the new Parliament. It would give schools extra cash for taking in pupils from disadvantaged areas. With the government committing itself to austerity measures to balance the books, there were queries about how the Department for Education (as it had been renamed after Labour's flirtation with the Department for Children, Schools and Families – famously dubbed the Department for Curtains and Soft Furnishing by Ed Balls in a bid to remember its initials) would pay for it. The answer was that Labour's ambitious £55 billion school rebuilding programme (Building Schools for the Future), under which every secondary school in the country would eventually receive a facelift, would be slashed. Back to the second Bill ushering in the pupil premium, though: it would also see reforms to the national curriculum to make it less prescriptive – academies and free schools were later given the right to ignore it altogether – and ushered in the promised reading test for six-year-olds designed to help schools identify struggling pupils earlier than they otherwise might have done. For good measure, Mr Gove played his part in igniting the "bonfire of the quangos" by announcing the abolition of the General Teaching Council set up by Labour, the Qualifications and Curriculum Authority, which monitored the national curriculum, and BECTA, set up to help schools with new technology. The GTC was supposed to have done a similar job for the teaching profession to that which the General Medical Council had done for doctors but Mr Gove argued that teachers had never "warmed to it" and it had only dismissed a handful of teachers for being incompetent in its time.

With the wrangling over the setting-up of the government following the election of a hung Parliament, there was little time to try and head off the boycott of the SATs national curriculum tests for 11-year-olds, which duly went ahead with the result that up to half the primary schools in the country found themselves unable to deliver the tests. Eventually, Mr Gove managed to persuade headteachers to call off their boycott for the following year with the promise of an independent review of SATs. In a letter to Russell Hobby, general secretary of the NAHT, Mr Gove acknowledged that the present arrangements "lead too many schools to drill children for tests".

Within two months of taking office, Christine Gilbert, Labour's appointment as Chief Inspector of Schools and head of Ofsted, announced her intention to quit and not seek a second term of office. Her departure had been widely foreseen.

It was known that Mr Gove, for one, was anxious to secure her departure – largely because of her links to Labour (she was married to a Labour MP). It paved the way for Mr Gove to make his own appointment: the mercurial Sir Michael Wilshaw, the headteacher at Mossbourne Academy in Hackney, who had an enviable record in getting pupils into Oxbridge. The school was on the site of the notorious Hackney Downs School – the first state school to be closed because of under-performance. The two Michaels may have been perceived as a marriage made in heaven at first but when it became clear that Sir Michael was going to be just as critical of under-performance in academies and free schools as in maintained schools, indeed any part of the education sector, relations between the two soured.

In an essay to mark Mr Gove's first 100 days in office, I observed: "Michael has distinct hyperactive tendencies as anyone who has come into contact him cannot fail to notice. Within three weeks of his arrival, he had decided to revolutionise the whole schools system. He wrote to every school in the land suggesting they consider opting out of local authority control and consider instead academy status." On the abolition of the quangos, I argued: "He sometimes acts without thinking of the consequences of what he has done. Someone, for instance, will still have to keep an eye on monitoring the curriculum; and there really should be a regulatory body that can keep pornographers, paedophiles, incompetents and violent people out of the profession (even if we would hope it could tackle more than 17 cases of incompetence a year)."

The Gove rush did not abate, though. By early September, 16 proposals for new free schools had been approved – reigniting fears that they would usher in a new breed of faith schools and create more segregation between religions (the 16 included five with a faith connection). To counteract this, Mr Gove announced that free faith schools would only be able to admit 50 per cent of their intake on grounds of their religion. Amongst those given the go-ahead was a project by author and journalist Toby Young to open a secondary school in Acton, west London, which would concentrate on the classics, with every pupil expected to learn Latin at least up until GCSE level. Two of the projects were proposed by the education charity ARK, set up by hedge fund millionaire Arpad Busson, which was gaining a good reputation for its sponsorship of academies and its ability to turn round the schools it was sponsoring.

The next furore – which Mr Gove was happy to tackle – stemmed from criticism of the exam boards. In a book published in the autumn, Mick Waters, the former head of curriculum at the QCA, claimed that the current system for A-levels and exam boards was "diseased" and "almost corrupt". "I used to think that all this criticism of exams that they were being dumbed down was unfair," he said, "but we've got a set of awarding bodies that are in a market place. I've seen people from awarding bodies talk to headteachers implying their examinations are easier." The upshot of this and similar claims that exams were becoming easier reinforced Mr Gove's belief that a review of exams was necessary. One of the changes he sought to make was that a single exam board should be responsible for delivery of each subject. All would be allowed to bid but only one would win the contract. For some teachers' leaders, that did not go far enough. They wanted a single exam board for the entire system – an aspiration I had some sympathy with. Mr Gove's idea floundered, though. There was a feeling that once the contract was awarded to one group, the other exam boards would simply cease to keep on staff trained in that subject so effectively you were awarding a contract for life. Other measures to toughen up on exam procedure were agreed later on in the 2010-15 Parliament, though.

One other initiative that was launched during this hectic introduction to the Coalition government's education policy was the English Baccalaureate, under which all schools would be ranked in exam league tables according to the percentage of pupils who obtained five A* to C grades at GCSE in five key academic subject areas: English, maths, the sciences, a language (ancient or modern) and the humanities (history or geography). The idea behind this initiative was obvious: to encourage better uptake of academic subjects rather than opting for subjects considered easier, such as media studies. To that end, it worked, as for the first few years it halted the decline in the number of pupils studying language and actually triggered a rise in this previously badly neglected subject area. There was criticism, though, that the place of arts and drama would be demoted in the curriculum. Religious studies, which has seen one of the biggest rises in uptake in recent years as young people sought to try and understand about different faiths, would be squeezed. Technology was also initially left out although eventually it was found a place under the sciences. One of the lesser-predicted outcomes of this initiative was that heads started switching their pupils away from subject areas they were studying in mid course to try and meet the new criteria (the English Baccalaureate measure was to be introduced in the following year's league tables). The rise in uptake of languages (and science) was to be welcomed, though. The only criticism was that, despite it being called the English Baccalaureate, it was not as broad as the International Baccalaureate. Later on, though, league tables were revised again to take account of students' performances in eight subject areas at GCSE – a move which would encourage them to study a wider range of subject areas.

So ended the first few hectic months of the Gove revolution.

*****

Given the fervour of those first few months of Michael Gove in office, it is perhaps surprising to note that higher education hit the headlines more in the first year of the Coalition government than primary and secondary schooling.

That was, of course, as a result of tuition fees – the issue which had prompted a truce between Labour and the Conservatives during the election period (because of the inquiry into student finance by Lord Browne) but ultimately led to the downfall of the Liberal Democrats who had opposed any rise in fees yet ended up helping to usher through rises of up to £9,000 a year. It was the issue which probably caused the Lib Dems to suffer most at the hands of the electorate as they sought to justify their change of heart.

First things first, though. It could have been much worse for the students in terms of what they had to pay. Lord Browne's report recommended universities be allowed to charge unlimited fees – and some of the more elite universities were indicating this could mean rises up to £12,000 a year.

What he was clear on, though, was that if a university wanted to charge more than £6,000 a year they would have to get permission from OFFA, the fair admissions watchdog, by convincing it that their plans would not deny access to disadvantaged students *ie* that there would be bursaries and other forms of aid on hand to help them. There was also help in the form of a maintenance grant of £3,250 a year for students whose family earnings were less than £60,000 a year. Graduates also would not have to start repaying the loans until they were earning £21,000 a year (as opposed to £15,000 under the previous system). Vince Cable, described by one of *The Independent's* political pundits as his party's "most beloved figure", announced the recommendations in the Commons.

Eventually, a compromise was reached which allowed Deputy Prime Minister Nick Clegg and enough Liberal Democrats to support the deal. It meant universities could charge up to £9,000 a year. Universities Minister David Willetts was insisting that only a handful of universities would charge the full whack and the average fee would probably be in the region of £7,000 a year. On the day of the announcement of the Browne inquiry's findings, I have to admit that I speculated that the average fee would be between £6,000 and £7,000 a year. Gradually, though, it became clear that almost all universities would be charging the maximum. It made the UK state higher education system the costliest in the world (Ivy League universities in the US charged more but the average for the whole country was slightly lower) in terms of students' contributions towards their university education.

The headlines, of course, were stolen by the students themselves – two large demonstrations in the centre of London turned violent. Students occupied Millbank and climbed up to the top of the building to make a rooftop protest. Police came in for criticism for what the students claimed were heavy-handed tactics – demonstrators were "kettled" in Trafalgar Square, unable to leave for hours.

So what of the reaction from would-be graduates? Well, the inevitable happened. A surge in applications for September 2011 – the last year before the new fees regime was introduced (in line with what had happened with top-up fees when Labour was in power). There was an upsurge in applications to study abroad, where fees were cheaper. Maastricht University, in particular, noted a rise in applications from the UK, its fees of £1,500 a year for UK undergraduates looking entirely reasonable. Schools re-ordered their priorities to ensure they had someone on the staff who could advise students on their overseas options. One such school was Hockerill Anglo-European College in Bishop's Stortford, Hertfordshire. The 830-pupil school appointed a student counsellor with the sole aim of helping students apply overseas. It also appointed a marketing company to scour the top 40 universities ranked worldwide for details of all the courses they offered to teach through the medium of English. The students were well-equipped to study abroad – the college offered seven different languages as part of its curriculum and put its pupils in for the International Baccalaureate rather than A-levels.

The change in the fees structure ushered in a new type of relationship between students and their higher education institution. They were pouring over league tables to see which universities had the best record for helping their students secure employment. Step forward the University of Worcester, which had seen 93 per cent of its students go into employment within six months of leaving, placing it higher in the rankings than Oxford and its Russell Group neighbours, Birmingham and Warwick. Business students, for instance, spent a year on paid work placements during a four-year course. The university placed great emphasis on equipping students for the world of work.

In addition, many companies were recruiting students straight from schools – and allowing them to take their degrees whilst on their payroll. The argument behind this was that the firms would have a graduate who was far more used to them by the time they had finished their university course – they would know what was expected of them rather than have to be taught anew the demands of a job like those students who signed up for employment only when they had graduated. KPMG announced a radical scheme: paying its students £20,000 a year while taking its degree courses. The scheme worked like this: 18-year-olds would sign a six-year contract, splitting their first four years between attending university and working in the company's offices. They would then be guaranteed two years of work with KPMG – by the end of which they would be earning £46,000 a year.

In the long term, this meant that student numbers in the UK rose again (once again the numbers of disadvantaged students applying to university grew, although there was still a considerable gap in percentage terms between their numbers and the numbers from more affluent families).

Within a couple of years of the £9,000-a-year fees regime, there were mutterings from members of the Russell Group of universities that they needed to charge even higher fees. Professor Andrew Hamilton, vice-chancellor of Oxford University argued that fees should be more in line with the cost of providing its courses, which was £16,000 a year. Most of the money from existing fees had to be used to offset government cutbacks, he argued.

There was no appetite for a further fees increase before the 2015 General Election in political circles, though. After the election, Jo Johnson, the new Universities Minister, put forward proposals to rank lecturers according to their teaching standards and said that those universities with a good ranking for teaching should be allowed to increase fees. However, as the increase would only be by the level of inflation (which was keeping stubbornly low) it was felt in university circles this would be unlikely to have a major effect on what students were charged.

At any rate, by far the biggest problem facing ministers was over the repayment of student loans. A report by the independent Higher Education Commission warned that the current fees-and-funding system was "unsustainable" and that three-quarters of graduates would be unlikely to be able to repay their loans by the 30-year cut-off period for repayments. Forecasters said the government was likely to have to spend more of taxpayers' money on higher education – much of it to pay for the non-repayment of loans – than it did before student loans were introduced. The changes, then, were hardly likely to meet their original purpose: that students should take more of the responsibility for paying the cost of their education than before.

The controversy ensured fees still became an issue during the 2015 General Election campaign with Labour leader Ed Miliband promising to cut them to £6,000 a year. However, he failed to get elected and the likelihood is there will be no increase or decrease during the lifetime of this Parliament, except for the possible modest increase in line with inflation proposed for the universities with the best teaching standards.

*****

Meanwhile, the Gove revolution in schools carried on apace. His first target of 2011 was to launch a revamp of the National Curriculum. It was to be a more traditionally based model concentrating on "academic rigour". In history, that meant more of a focus on individuals such as Churchill, Nelson and Wellington. In geography, it moved away from issues like global warming and climate change with the document arguing that the curriculum "should not become a vehicle for imposing passing political fads on our children". His reforms coincided with a new wave of unrest in the teaching profession over the government's austerity measures as first the traditionally moderate Association of Teachers and Lecturers and then the National Association of Head Teachers staged strike action over government plans to reduce their pensions – not something within the remit of the Department for Education but symptomatic of a worsening relationship between the government and the unions. Headteachers also warned that the squeeze on school budgets – which meant funding for 16 to 19 education failed to be covered by the Coalition's pledge to protect spending – was already leading to some subjects being dropped from the curriculum on offer at A-level, in particular languages.

Meanwhile, the government's first 24 free schools opened in the autumn term with David Cameron predicting there would be "hundreds more" in the ensuing few years. In an intriguing interview with *The Independent*, journalist and author Toby Young – the founder of one of the first to be opened – warned it would be difficult for parents' groups like the one which had campaigned for the West London Free School to run their own schools in future. Ministers had tightened up on the rules governing the operation of free schools, making it almost essential that any potential bidder would need the support of professional education consultants to help them plot their way through all the bureaucracy. "I think it is a shame," he said. "I think one of the virtues of the free school policy is that it involves parents in the ongoing life of the school. All the research suggests the more involved they are in their children's education the better the children do. ARK, E-ACT and the Harris Foundation (private sponsors of schools) are all good at running schools but at the end of the day the free school movement should be about mavericks like us setting up an innovative school rather than academy sponsors setting up a chain of 13 schools that are one of a kind."

I have to say I support much of what he was saying and believe that free schools should be about something that is innovative rather than the routine method for providing education. As a result I found myself backing a plan for a pioneering free school that got turned down by the bureaucrats. It aimed to break the link between teenagers and the gang culture that can surround them. It was to be called Diaspora High School, in Lewisham, south London, and was the brainchild of two black teachers who worked in the area, Kay Johnston and Anne Broni. They aimed to guarantee all their pupils three months' work experience after finishing their schooling to avoid them going on the dole and ending up on the streets. It won the support of Dr Michael Hrebeniak, director of English studies and senior admissions tutor at Wolfson College, Cambridge, who was set to become a governor at the school and help provide master classes for pupils who aspired to go to universities like his. He was withering in his criticism of the government's decision to axe the project, describing the entire free school programme as a "lousy commercial sham" created by the Conservatives to benefit middle-class parents and religious groups. He said the two teachers behind the project had "50 years of experience as transformative teachers in inner city schools". "In keeping with their enviable sense of probity and dignity, Ms Johnston and Ms Broni would perhaps not bring themselves to muster the charges of racism and sexism in response to your department's inexplicably contemptuous behaviour towards them," he said in a letter to Mr Gove. "I, nonetheless, would have no such qualms." Officials, he said, had indicated they felt there was a question mark over whether the applicants could deliver the plan as they had limited experience of school leadership.

There were, of course, other examples of innovative success stories – including a couple of bilingual primary schools, one teaching through the medium of English and German and the other through English and Spanish, which gave pupils the bedrock they needed in languages at an early age. A school that also impressed me was Langley Park, a primary free school in Reading, which was using the free schools' freedom to hire non-qualified teachers (to become one of the key controversies between Labour and the Conservatives as the next election approached) to teach arts and drama. It was the article I wrote about these schools that led to Mr Gove describing me as a "brilliant" journalist in the Commons. I suspect that at the end of the day I did not quite retain that billing in his eyes. Actually, I know.

It was about this time that Mr Gove went to war with those who opposed his reforms – in particular singling out those who opposed his compulsory academisation programme for failing or struggling schools as being "happy with failure" and "enemies of promise". He appeared to have shifted a gear from the man who went to an NAHT conference after his first year in office, addressing them after motion after motion had been critical of government reforms, but who won them over with a calculated speech as to how he was to reform the national curriculum tests and put improving the lot of disadvantaged students at the top of his agenda. As time wore on, he seemed to weary of trying to keep people on board for his reforms – and just wanted to forge ahead with them with breakneck speed. One reason I heard to explain this was that he felt the Conservatives only had one term to reform the education system – and so could not spare the time to bring those he considered backsliders along. The "enemies of promise" comment was then followed by liking academics and senior education officials to "The Blob" – a shivering ameoba which appeared in a B-movie starring Steve McQueen in the 1950s and ate human beings. Among those dismissed as "The Blob" were 100 academics who signed a letter to *The Independent* complaining that his proposed curriculum was too "Gradgrind" in its philosophy and would squeeze creativity out of the school timetable – legitimate comments shared in some measure by John Cridland, of the CBI, which was pursuing a campaign to get schools to produce more "rounded and grounded" human beings than just victims of an "exam factory" approach.

Mr Gove's next target was the examination system. He wanted to toughen up GCSEs and A-levels and return to the traditional system of relying on the two-hour end-of-course exam rather than coursework done during the year. His comments did follow 27 consecutive years of rises in the A-level pass rate – a factor which had led growing numbers of voices to query whether the exams were really helping to indicate high flyers as so many achieved top-grade passes. Under his reforms, he said, "there will be years when, because we're going to make exams tougher, the number of people passing will fall."

To that end, Mr Gove's supporters announced through a leak to the *Daily Mail* (most of his reforms found their way to public consumption through leaks to the *Daily Mail* or *Daily Telegraph*) that their master planned to replace GCSEs with "explicitly harder" old-style O-level exams in English, maths, physics, chemistry and biology. For those "less intelligent" pupils, there would be easier CSE-style exams which critics feared would have an adverse effect on social mobility. The plan had been put forward without any discussion with Mr Gove's Coalition partners in government – indeed Deputy Prime Minister Nick Clegg was away at an international summit in Brazil. As soon as he got to hear of it, he instructed senior Liberal Democrat party officials in a heated telephone call to oppose the idea. In a statement, he said: "I'm not in favour of anything that would lead to a two-tier system where children at quite a young age are somehow cast on a scrapheap. What you want is an exam system which is fit for the future, doesn't turn the clock back to the past and rewards hard work for the many ... and not just for the few." Other voices were raised against the idea from within the Conservative Party including former Education Secretary Lord (Kenneth) Baker and Graham Stuart, chairman of the Commons select committee on education. Lord Baker argued that the CSE had become a "valueless piece of paper", not recognised by potential employers. "So don't resurrect a failure," he added. There was nothing else for it – Mr Gove had to drop the idea although he had at least put down a marker to the right of the party that he was their ally when it came to reforms. At this stage he was denying he had any interest in leading the party or becoming Prime Minister. Subsequent events, though, appeared to change his mind (although his shafting of Boris Johnson after the Brexit referendum ensured he never had the opportunity to press forward with his change of heart).

Mr Gove got his way with the GCSE results in the summer of 2012 – there was a fall in the percentage of pupils getting five A* to C grade passes. This was largely as a result of exams regulator Ofqual putting pressure on the exam boards to raise the C/D grade boundary between the January and June sittings on the grounds that it appeared the pass mark for a C grade was too generous. It meant that a pupil sitting the exam in the summer had to score higher marks than one taking it in January, which headteachers considered grossly unfair and demanded an inquiry into what had happened. A subsequent court case ruled, though, that Ofqual had been right in its assessment.

Meanwhile, Mr Gove came up with his "son of O-level" proposal for reforming the GCSE exam – which was to replace it with an English Baccaulaureate: like the EBacc measure for the performance tables with those who gained top grade passes in five core academic subjects (English, maths, science, a language and a humanities subject – history or geography) qualifying for it. Once again, though, Mr Gove found few takers for his idea even in the private sector of education where he might have thought it would be backed and was forced into a climbdown. The Girls' School Association, in the shape of Louise Robinson, its president and headmistress of Merchant Taylors' Girls' School, an independent school in Crosby, near Liverpool, argued against the idea, saying that instead of preparing pupils for the world with a 1960s-style curriculum and exam structure, we should be looking ahead to the world of the 2020s and 2030s. The Commons select committee on education claimed in a report that the government "has not proved its case that GCSEs in the key academic subjects should be abolished". It added that Mr Gove was "trying to do too much, too quickly and we call on the government to balance the pace of reform and get it right". Nearly 100 arts organisations, including the National Theatre and Royal Philharmonic Society, signed a letter claiming that the English Baccalaureate would squeeze creativity out of the curriculum at a time when the creative industries were among the most vibrantly successful economic forces in the country. In his U-turn, Mr Gove announced a new measure for ranking schools on their pupils' progress in their top eight subjects – thus giving hope of a boost in take-up of the arts and drama. However, allies of Mr Gove argued he would not be too upset by what was left of his plans – there would be a move away from coursework to testing pupils in end-of-course exams and the exams would be tougher. One ally conceded: "There was a failure to establish a coalition of support for the idea and he (Mr Gove) became more isolated. The education establishment is violently hostile." The source added: "We have still done 80 to 90 per cent of what we wanted to achieve with this package and will be able to make a real difference to the quality of exams."

It was about this time that I became part of the story of the friction between Mr Gove and the education world (I have never considered that my job makes me part of the education world – merely an observer of it). *The Independent* had run a piece emanating from headteachers in Lancashire who complained they were being "bribed" to become academies which was written by a colleague of mine, James Cusick. I had written a comment to go with it which backed their complaints. Most of the wrath from the story fell upon James Cusick but in an email to my colleague, Mr Gove's controversial special adviser, Dominic Cummings, criticised my role in the affair. The upshot of a footnote to his email was that there was more disappointment than anger that I should be involved in the story. Subsequently, my colleague James unearthed another story alleging that an "intimidating culture" existed between Mr Gove's special advisers and civil servants. An internal grievance report for the Department for Education stated that the prevailing climate was "more reminiscent of an episode of *The Thick Of It* than a reflection of acceptable behaviour of employees of the Department for Education". I again wrote a comment on the piece in which I described Mr Gove as "unfailingly courteous and charming in his dealings with almost everyone", adding that "I also have not felt the wrath of a special adviser come down on me despite being critical on occasions – until this week". Cue a 3am email from Mr Cummings suggesting I should consult one of my education correspondent colleagues, Chris Cook from the *Financial Times*, about fixing an appointment with a therapist if I believed his comments counted as "wrath". Mr Cook had upset the Gove entourage with stories about their use of private email accounts for government business. (I thought I was being quite kind to him in comparison to other comments on the paper!) If I didn't need a therapist, he argued, I knew the piece was "absurd … because you know I never call and shout at you." He was right about the "never call" (I wasn't a member of the fully paid-up army of Gove supporters) and therefore there was no shouting either. He finished by saying: "I will be circulating my email to your colleagues so they know exactly what is behind your 'wrath' column." I thought that said more about him than me. If it was meant to intimidate, it failed. I came under pressure from MPs to lodge a complaint against him as – apparently – it is against a special adviser's code of conduct to insult a journalist. I found that almost unbelievable! I resisted – I saw no point in making a prolonged antagonistic case out of this. Instead, *The Independent* just published excerpts from the 3am email and the controversy it had caused, leaving readers to make up their own minds about what had happened. There were repercussions, though. Subsequently, I had all help from Mr Gove's aides withdrawn. I was negotiating a piece to be written by Mr Gove for our Easter education pages in which I had asked him to write about what he thought teachers should be debating at their conferences. I thought it could be quite an amusing piece. I was told there was "no chance" of it going ahead so I replaced it with a two-page spread on a book by former NASUWT general secretary Nigel de Gruchy extolling the virtues of "industrial action with a halo" over excluding disruptive children from the classroom. Talk about cutting your nose off to spite your face: Mr Gove's advisers could have had two pages of largely helpful publicity; instead, it went to a teachers' leader extolling the virtues of industrial action. I was later told that it had been indicated to my editor that there would be more balanced coverage of education in the paper were I to be replaced. He pointed out that I had written several articles praising successful free schools and academies as well as exposing the faults in others. A couple of years later I was also told that I was one of three education journalists on a "blacklist" not to be helped. Dominic Cummings, remember, was vetoed by Andy Coulson, the now disgraced director of communications for David Cameron (because of the 'phone tapping scandal'), for a post as Mr Gove's special adviser when the Coalition government took office. I am tempted to say that if Andy Coulson does not think you are fit enough for public office...

My conclusion about all this is a certain sadness that this is the way governments and their advisers conduct their affairs but I think what happened in this case goes to the heart of some of the faults in Mr Gove's regime. He could not brook criticism – witness the "Blob" comments and "enemies of promise" – and in the end saw no merit in trying to convince even the mildest critics in the education world of the necessity for his reforms.

Things went from bad to worse in terms of Mr Gove's relationship with the education world. Perhaps not surprisingly the NUT passed a motion of no confidence in Mr Gove at their Easter conference. It was followed a month later by a similar motion at the NAHT – an organisation less inclined to indulge in such moves. He was then heckled as he spoke. At one stage, he told a questioner: "I admire your candour but we are going to have to part company." A heckler shouted: "Are you leaving then?" There was loud laughter when Mr Gove said it was important to discover "the sources of the stress you are facing". Gerard Kelly, then editor of the *TES* who was chairing the session, remarked: "They think you're one of them."

Later in the year, Mike Nicholson, then head of admissions at Oxford University, warned that Mr Gove's exam reforms would "wreck" the English education system. He said there was "widespread concern" at changes to GCSEs and A-levels, which also were being made tougher and returning to a reliance on the end-of-course exam, adding: "The impact of bringing in both is just going to wreck the English education system." He particularly singled out the decision to make the AS-level a standalone qualification rather than count as halfway towards an A-level pass, saying it would have "tragic consequences" for the participation of disadvantaged students at university. He said there was "limited evidence" that any changes to A-levels were necessary.

There was some comfort for Mr Gove over his reforms, though. Exam league tables published early in 2014 showed a massive increase in the take-up of traditional academic subjects at GCSE level as a result of the introduction of his EBacc measure for ranking schools – a total of 72,000 more students were eligible for the qualification, a rise of more than 50 per cent on the previous year. The number of schools where more than 50 per cent of pupils achieved the EBacc also rose from 174 to 237.

There was another flashpoint with his coalition partners, though, as it was announced that Baroness (Sally) Morgan, a former aide to Tony Blair, had been dismissed as chair of education standards watchdog Ofsted. Sir Michael Wilshaw, the chief inspector, had pleaded with Mr Gove to keep her but the Education Secretary was adamant: he wanted someone fresh to push through reforms to the way Ofsted was run. His attempt to replace her with David Ross, a multimillionaire Conservative Party donor and a co-founder of Carphone Warehouse, only fuelled the controversy.

Then, as I drove through the Northamptonshire countryside on a well-deserved day off (why do these things always happen on a day off?), the news came through on my car radio: Michael Gove had gone. David Cameron had shifted him to become the party's Chief Whip. I turned around and headed for my computer.

TIMELINE

2010

NAHT and NUT boycott SATs tests.

Outstanding schools given the right to become academies.

Michael Gove launches EBacc measure to rank schools in exam league tables.

New reading test for six-year-olds to identify struggling pupils announced.

Government announces plan to allow universities to charge up to £9,000 a year in tuition fees.

2011

Teachers and heads strike over cuts to pensions.

First government free schools open.

Almost all universities say they will charge the maximum £9,000-a-year fee for courses.

2012

Mr Gove's aides announce plan to replace GCSEs with an exam along O-level lines – but it is withdrawn after Liberal Democrat opposition, whereupon Mr Gove replaces it with move to replace academic GCSEs with English Baccalaureate.

Exams regulator Ofqual plans to end year-on-year exam rises with policy of "comparative outcomes" which should link results to the previous year.

2013

Mr Gove forced to drop English Baccalaureate proposal – but goes ahead with plan to axe coursework in GCSE and focus on end-of-course examinations.

NUT and NAHT pass no-confidence motions in Mr Gove.

Oxford vice-chancellor calls for further rise in fees – saying they should move nearer the £16,000 cost of providing a course.

2014

Mr Gove sacks Baroness Morgan as chair of Ofsted, fuelling row with chief schools inspector Sir Michael Wilshaw, his Liberal Democrat Coalition partners and Labour.

Michael Gove reshuffled.

Chapter Nine
After The Lord Mayor's Show

One thing most pundits were agreed upon about Michael Gove's departure from the Department for Education – it was a surprise. Christine Blower, general secretary of the NUT, said she expected a smile may have formed on the lips of many a teacher when they heard of his departure because of his treatment they had received. It was another 'JFK moment' for education – most people could remember where they were when they heard that he had gone. (As I said, I was in a car driving to Northampton and performed as quick a U-turn as Mr Gove himself had over his plan to reintroduce old-style O-levels as I beetled back home to write his education epitaph.)

The reason, it appeared, that David Cameron decided he had to go was as a result of private polling presented to the Prime Minister by his Australian election strategist, Lynton Crosby, showing that Mr Gove had become deeply unpopular with teachers. "Toxic" was the expression used. Conservative Party strategists remembered that one of the reasons the party had failed to win the 2010 election outright was because too few people in the public services had voted for them. Add together teachers and their families and you have a constituency of well over one million voters. Also, Deputy Prime Minister Nick Clegg had indicated that the Liberal Democrats would have targeted Mr Gove at the election because they believed voters considered his policies to be unpopular. There was no love lost, in particular, between Mr Clegg and Mr Gove's special adviser Dominic Cummings and no lack of controversy between them. Mr Clegg had vetoed the O-level plan and helped to torpedo the idea of replacing core academic GCSEs with an English Baccalaureate qualification. He had opposed the dismissal of Baroness Morgan from her post at Ofsted and the Liberal Democrat Schools Minister David Laws had sought to put distance between his party and the Conservatives over Mr Gove's refusal to give Ofsted the powers to inspect academy chains – a power sought by Mr Gove's choice as chief schools inspector, Sir Michael Wilshaw. As providers of a large chunk of the education service, academy chains, argued Mr Laws, should be made available to public scrutiny. Mr Gove argued that Ofsted maintained the right to inspect all schools and did not need further powers. The Liberal Democrats would argue that, under an untrammelled Conservative government, policies like the introduction of the English Baccalaureate would rear their heads again and come to fruition.

Was it a demotion to move Mr Gove to Chief Whip? Absolutely not, said Mr Cameron. There was an important job to be done keeping the party together and singing from the same hymn sheet in the run-up to the General Election. However, there was the little matter of a £36,000 pay cut to take up his new post. Also, with hindsight, we hardly ever heard of Mr Gove in his role of Chief Whip in the run-up to the election.

In truth, Mr Gove had succeeded in getting the bulk of his reforms through the Commons. The academies programme had expanded so that now more than half the country's state secondary schools had academy status, the free school programme had got off the ground – with a couple of hiccups from schools that had failed their Ofsted inspections and closed. At one, Discovery School in Newcastle, inspectors said that pupils had not progressed at all in English over a year.

Exam reform was on the statute book – both GCSEs and A-levels now relied on the end-of-course exam rather than coursework, the questions had been made harder. In the summer just a month after his departure, Mr Gove got what he had predicted: the first drop in the pass rate for more than 30 years, coupled with a fall in top grade pass rates. One of the reasons cited for this was the introduction of his EBacc measure for ranking schools' performance which had led to them entering far more pupils (including pupils not necessarily noted for being high flyers) for core academic subjects. They found it harder to pass the exams. The results were described as "the Gove legacy results" by education pundits.

So teachers may have heaved a collective sigh of relief at Mr Gove's departure but what was to happen now? Well, education was put in the hands of Nicky

Morgan, whose promotion to one of the high profile departments of state came just four years after she had entered the Commons as an MP. She had joined the party as a teenager and won the marginal seat of Loughborough at a second attempt in 2010. The message from Mr Cameron was that the Gove reforms would carry on – it was to be business as usual – but Mrs Morgan was expected to be more amenable to meeting teachers' organisations and not conduct her ministry with the same disdain for critics that her predecessor had shown. It was, in essence, an instruction to keep the profile of education lower than it had been in the Gove years.

One of her first tasks on taking up the brief was to give the government's response to an inquiry her predecessor had set up into the so-called "Trojan Horse" affair in Birmingham. The controversy centred around a letter – widely thought to be a fake – outlining plots by extreme Islamists to take over the running of a number of schools in the city. In his report, former Metropolitan Police anti-terrorism head Peter Clarke said there was proof of such a plot. He said there was "clear evidence that there are a number of people, associated with each other and in positions of influence in schools and governing bodies (in Birmingham) who espouse, endorse or fail to challenge extremist views. There has been co-ordinated, deliberate and sustained action to introduce an intolerant and aggressive Islamist ethos". In one of his last acts, Mr Gove sought to put a new duty on teachers to teach "British values" to their pupils. The move created controversy because many felt the values he was talking about – such as respect for other pupils – were not uniquely British. However, in her Commons statement, Mrs Morgan went further, ordering the National Council for Teaching and Leadership to determine whether any teachers identified by the Clarke inquiry had been guilty of misconduct and should be barred from the profession. She stressed that any actions that "undermine fundamental British values" should be viewed as "misconduct". In addition, she made it clear that exposing pupils to extremist speakers "should be regarded as a failure to protect pupils and British values" and be treated with an immediate suspension.

The ramifications of the Trojan Horse affair continued, though, spreading to London where one Church of England school in Tower Hamlets, the Sir John Cass's Foundation and Red Coat Church of England school, for long rated 'outstanding' by inspectors, had its rating reduced to 'inadequate' after Ofsted found it had failed to monitor the activities of a sixth-form debating society at the school which had a Facebook site with links to hard-line Islamist preachers. According to Ofsted, that constituted a failure to safeguard its pupils. There was talk of similar situations existing in other parts of the country – notably Bradford – but evidence never emerged on the scale it had done in Birmingham.

Mrs Morgan's insistence on cracking down on ensuring "British values" were taught in schools may have earned her some enemies. (After all, it was argued, democracy and a respect for other people's points of view and religions weren't uniquely British.) However, the controversy never reignited to the extent that it impinged upon her popularity.

Her next task was to preside over the free schools programme continuing apace with a further 80 opening their doors in the September after she took office. They joined 174 that had already opened. In addition, there were 13 new University Technical Colleges – a new breed of 14-to-19 schools pioneered by former Education Secretary Lord (Kenneth) Baker offering a first-class vocational education to help pupils pursue their future careers. One such was the Sir Charles Kao UTC in Harlow, Essex, where the students would spend the first few weeks not at their desks but on a life-like work experience project not dissimilar to an episode from the BBC TV show, *The Apprentice*. The UTC also had links with the Princess Alexandra Hospital in Harlow and the pupils would be devising knee joints designed to last their patients 20 years – one of which would be chosen for development after the students had gone before a board at the college to explain their design.

There was still controversy over the free school and academies programme, though. In particular, a survey of 12 schools run by the Academies Enterprise Trust (one of the country's larger academy chains) by Ofsted showed too many of its pupils were failing to receive an adequate education. Matthew Coffey, Ofsted's chief operating officer, said in a letter to the Trust: "Around half the academies in the trust are not yet good." It followed on from comments in Peter Clarke's "Trojan Horse" report which pointed out that some schools facing a takeover by hardline Islamists were academies and added: "The autonomy granted to those who run academies can make those institutions vulnerable to those without good intentions." The warnings were largely unheeded in ministerial circles.

For her part, Mrs Morgan – in a noted difference of style to many of her predecessors – dealt with the controversies in a fairly low-key way without inflaming the profession. In fact, she initiated discussions with teachers' leaders, who were made more welcome than at any time under her predecessor. She even took on the task of trying to placate them on one issue that they had been complaining about for years – their workload – at one stage offering the opportunity for teachers to contact her department via email with comments about it. She was flooded with comments – some 44,000 teachers replied, creating their own workload headache for her department – and took some steps to try and improve their situation, acknowledging that the government and other bodies like Ofsted should not introduce changes to exams, inspections *etc* mid-year. It was not enough for the teachers' leaders but at least it gave the impression she was trying to meet some of their demands.

The first real sign of any controversy came in an unexpected way when she was addressing the launch of the 'Your Life' campaign which set itself a target of aiming for a 50 per cent increase in the number of teenagers opting for maths and physics in the next three years. Teenagers, she argued, should steer away from the arts and humanities and opt for maths or science subjects if they wanted to access the widest range of jobs. "If you wanted to do something or even if you didn't know what you wanted to do, then the arts and humanities were what you chose because they were useful for all types of jobs," she said of the past. "Of course we know now that couldn't be further from the truth – that the subjects that keep young people's options open and unlock the door to all sorts of careers are the STEM subjects (science, technology, engineering and maths)." The comments infuriated supporters of the humanities with Nigel Carrington, vice-chancellor of the University of the Arts London, arguing: "This absurd discrimination between 'hard' STEM subjects and 'soft' arts subjects will damage the next generation of entrepreneurs. The government needs to recognise that creativity is vital to the economy and should be taught." It was, however, a one-day controversy and Mrs Morgan was largely successful in her aim of managing to keep controversies under control in the advent of the election campaign.

The opening shots in the election campaign were fired well in advance of its official start by the opposition. In fact, Tristram Hunt, Labour's education spokesman, floated one of his key policies – a pledge to give more emphasis in schools to developing attributes like 'character' and 'resilience' in young pupils – a year beforehand. His aim was to move schools away from the "exams factory" model which had come under widespread criticism in recent years. Mr Hunt, though, emphasized it was not an "either/or" situation – and that time spent developing a child's well-being could have a spin off in improving their academic attainment at the same time. It would help them enjoy school. He also said it was time to start teaching pupils concentration skills – as the age of the internet and social media had eroded them. "They (the pupils) need to learn the ability to concentrate for sustained periods –, especially in today's world of short attention spans," he said. "I think young people need help with being able to do that." The cudgel on this issue was also taken up by Nicky Morgan – although she made more of a link between developing pupils' character and discipline and argued that persuading ex-armed services personnel to take up posts in schools could help in this direction. For his part, Mr Hunt rejected what he called the "Gordonstoun cold showers" approach to character building – a reference to the Scottish independent school attended by generations of the Royal Family. I must confess I found it refreshing that politicians were talking for once about more than just standards, crackdowns on discipline, target setting and school structures – and in the run-up to an election campaign. We will never know how Tristram Hunt would have developed this theme on taking office but, suffice it to say, it does not seem to have maintained the national prominence it gained during the campaign. The "exams factory" approach has not been buried or forgotten.

Otherwise, the big difference between the two main parties was over the Conservatives' free school programme, with David Cameron pledging 500 more schools in the lifetime of the next Parliament while Mr Hunt called for an end to the experiment. There were clashes, too, over the government's decision to allow academies and free schools to appoint non-qualified teaching staff and its plans to extend this right to all schools. Both Labour and the Liberal Democrats sought a trained teacher in every classroom. David Laws, the Liberal Democrat Schools Minister, admitted that the government's policy of encouraging the use of non-qualified staff had slipped by on his watch but added that he did not agree with it. Figures showed that the rise of the free school movement had seen a growth in the number of unqualified teachers in schools. Intriguingly, the only party campaigning for a return to selection and grammar schools – an issue which provoked silence from the main protagonists at least as far as manifestos were concerned – was UKIP.

Labour also stuck with Ed Miliband's pledge to reduce student fees to £6,000 a year. It had to be said, overall, that, compared with the 1997 "education, education, education" campaign, the issue hardly took off at the hustings.

Public spending was also a battleground with different pledges from the parties – the Conservatives pledged to maintain school spending for 5 to 16-year-olds although Mr Cameron acknowledged this did not necessarily mean it would keep pace with inflation. Labour said it would ensure no real term cuts in spending and extended the pledge to the entire education system, *ie* including sixth-forms which had borne the brunt of the cuts during the past five years – particularly to A-level courses at sixth-form colleges. Nick Clegg promised that education spending would be a "red line" in any negotiations over a coalition with any party. He said he would like to see education spending rising from £49 billion to £55.3 billion during the lifetime of the new Parliament – in effect promising to spend £2.5 billion more than Labour and £5 billion more than the Conservatives.

In the end, the result – a Conservative overall victory – gave David Cameron and Nicky Morgan, who was retained as Education Secretary, *carte blanche* to carry on with their policies.

*****

Not long after the election, news came through that the former chief schools inspector Sir Chris Woodhead had died at the age of 68. In the latter years of his life he suffered from motor neurone disease and was paralysed from the neck downwards. He made it clear that – if his life became unbearable – he would not want to prolong it. As to how he would like to die, he put it this way: "The truth is I would be more likely to drive my wheelchair off a cliff in Cornwall than go to Dignitas and speak to a bearded social worker over my future." His mind, though, was still as sharp as ever, as I discovered when I went to interview him about nine months before his death. One thing struck me about that interview – he still had a wicked sense of humour and a wry smile formed on his lips as he contemplated one of the unexpected consequences of his illness. "For my opponents who thought when they heard I had got motor neurone disease – 'ah well, that's the end of him, then' – I've got news for them," he said. "They're wrong. In fact, it's made me concentrate more on it (education). I had been planning to do things like gardening and rock climbing but obviously I can't now." He spoke enthusiastically about his plans to become an academy sponsor and revealed he already had one school in Cumbria in his sights for take-over. He also devoted his latter years to running a company called Cognita, which had as its broad aim making private education affordable to a larger range of families.

No one could ever claim he was anything but a polarising influence on education – hated by the teaching organisations for the harsh words he had to say about their members' performance. His first public utterance was to say he believed there were 15,000 incompetent teachers in state school classrooms and he considered it his job to get rid of them. He, more than anyone else, set the tone for how education standards watchdog Ofsted went about its business. He wasn't the first chief inspector under the new regime but his predecessor, Professor Stuart Sutherland, only lasted long enough to set the organisation up. He was stern in his criticism when he felt schools or teachers were falling short of the demanding standards they should be attaining. Teachers felt Ofsted was quick to apportion blame but – to a generation brought up under the HMI regime – they also criticised the fact that Ofsted did not see it as part of its role to help those schools that it had criticised to improve. Sir Chris's sympathies lay with the Conservative right but – for a time – he forged a working relationship with Tony Blair's first Education Secretary David Blunkett whom he said he saw as part of the movement to improve standards. In fact, he was so identified with the right that I can remember one of the frostiest moments at an NAHT conference was in 1997 – just after Labour had swept back into power – when it became clear that Mr Blunkett did not intend to sack him as chief schools inspector.

As far as Sir Chris's supporters were concerned, he had inherited a situation at Ofsted in which little more than half of the pupils in primary school reached the required standards in English and maths in their national curriculum test at 11 before going on to secondary school. It was his attempts to expose the lack of basic literacy skills that made him indispensable when Tony Blair took office in 1997. The Prime Minister, who had won power on his "education, education, education" slogan could hardly sack someone who was a strong supporter of improving standards.

Controversy followed him throughout his working life – including allegations that he had an affair with a schoolgirl while she was still one of his pupils. He insisted the affair (they went on to live with each other for several years) had started after she had left school. Details of the relationship emerged after Sir Chris had been caught on tape telling teacher trainees that sex with a pupil could be "experiential and educative on both sides".

Most politicians would agree that schools needed the extra scrutiny that Ofsted – under Sir Chris – brought to the system but it is interesting to note how the service developed after he left office. His successor, Sir Mike Tomlinson, made it clear in an interview with me as he succeeded him: "I am not Chris Woodhead." These were the words that teachers wanted to hear rather than any discussion of the educational policies he sought to pursue whilst at Ofsted. Ofsted never became the teachers' friend but Sir Mike and his successors Sir David Bell and Christine Gilbert did turn it into less of an ogre in the eyes of teachers than it had been. The nearest to Sir Chris in style was Sir Michael Wilshaw, the only one knighted for his services to education before he took up his role at Ofsted as a result of turning round the fortunes of the inner city Mossbourne Academy in Hackney, east London, and making Oxbridge a realistic target for disadvantaged students. He was different, though, as Michael Gove came to find out. You wouldn't call him a voice of the right – he was even-handed in his criticism, pointing out the shortcomings of academy chains and free schools as well as the maintained sector. Too even-handed, it seems for Michael Gove and even Nicky Morgan couldn't resist a dig at him when confirming the appointment of his successor Amanda Spielman, late of the Ark academy chain and exam regulator Ofqual. Mrs Morgan was in hot water with members of the Commons education select committee who expressed "concerns" about Ms Spielman's ability to do the job. However, in, confirming her appointment, she conceded "there might not be so many headlines" as a result of Ms Spielman's approach but added that she would not be cowed in making her opinions felt if she had the evidence to back them up. It remains to be seen how Ms Spielman approaches her job – but I think there was probably a good deal of wishful thinking in Mrs Morgan's comments about the lack of headlines. Ofsted therefore may be entering a more bureaucratic phase with a leader more concerned with administrative efficiency in the inspection regime than exposing the flaws in the system. If it veers too heavily in that direction, it would be a pity.

*****

There were rumours around during the election campaign that, once the vote had been done and dusted, and if the Conservatives returned to power, David Cameron would thank Nicky Morgan for keeping education quiet as an issue up until the election, move her on to some other cabinet post and replace her with a right-wing zealot in the Michael Gove mould. It did not happen: Nicky Morgan had done well in keeping the issue under the radar – helped by a teaching profession whose leaders did not feel their members were ready for further industrial action – and it was felt she deserved a second stab at the job.

The big issue of the 2015 Parliament was to be a further expansion of the academies and free school programme with Mr Cameron declaring as his first target the creation of 500 new free schools by the next election. It was significant that he included in this the University Technical Colleges pioneered by Lord Baker. Under Michael Gove's reign, the UTCs – and new Career Colleges, based on the same philosophy as the UTCs but making use of the further education sector to deliver a career-based vocational education – did not have pride of place in his affections. George Osborne was a fan, though, and the tide now seemed to be turning in favour of them.

In addition, Mr Cameron also wanted an expansion of the academies programme and, within a year of the election, the government announced its aim (through Mr Osborne's budget of forcing every state school in the country to become an academy by 2022). It was hardly surprising that this announcement was opposed by every teachers' organisation in the land and, the following week when the NUT conference opened, by Labour leader Jeremy Corbyn in a ground-breaking appearance at the conference. It was the first time the leader of a political party had addressed the NUT. He described it as "the asset stripping of our education facilities" and vowed that Labour would fight the proposal. "Children are facing rising class sizes, there is a shortage of teachers and parents already face a crisis in school places," he said. "The forced academisation will do nothing to address any of these problems. And yet £700 million will need to be found to fund this needless organisation that fails to address a single issue that matters to teachers, parents and pupils." The Labour leader won a standing ovation from the conference; one delegate cried "I love you, Jeremy" as he made his way to the rostrum. Motions had been tabled for later on, over the Easter weekend, warning of industrial action if the government continued to go down this path. This was a sentiment repeated at the much less militant Association of Teachers and Lecturers conference the following week where Schools Minister Nick Gibb got a very different reception to that given to Mr Corbyn. There were shouts of "total crap" and "bollocks" from moderately-minded teachers when he sought to defend the proposal.

Yet I remember thinking at the NUT conference this was not really the most important opposition to the plan. My eye had been caught by a press release from the Bow Group, a pressure group within the Conservative party, emailed to me just before Mr Corbyn started speaking, which talked of the proposal going against basic Conservative values that parents should be allowed to choose their children's school. That coupled with the fact that it was opposed by Conservative leaders of local education authorities – who felt they were running successful education systems and could not see why they should be forced into parting company with their schools. Many Conservative backbench MPs also felt the same way and it began to look as if the government would struggle to get the measure through the House of Commons, especially as there was further controversy over its attempt ,announced in the same breath, to remove the obligation on schools to have parents on their governing bodies. It was, to recall the interview I had done with Toby Young at the start of the free school programme, an indication that, far from promoting "parent power" and giving parents more say in the running of their children's schools, the day of the professional private sponsors was coming to the education system in spades. Eventually, the crescendo of opposition from within its own grass roots supporters became too great and the government was forced into a U-turn, dropping the idea that every school should become an academy. Thus ended, it seemed, the big debate of the last 30 years. It had started with schools opting out of local authority control with both John Major's and Tony Blair's governments arguing at times that they wanted to see every state school run along the lines of those in the private sector. Always the opposition to this idea was too great. In fact, evidence was produced by Ofsted that schools stood a better chance of moving out of special measures more quickly if they remained with the local authority rather than opting for academy status. Of course, the U-turn did not preclude an expansion of the academies programme – struggling schools could still be forced to embrace academisation. There would probably be battles ahead over the future of individual schools but the wholesale academisation of the entire system was now on the back burner.

Earlier in the lifetime of this Parliament, Mr Osborne had made another foray into education policy by announcing that maintenance grants for university would be abolished by September 2016.

One issue that never went away during the 36 years I covered the national education beat was selection. The country appeared to have been at a stalemate for years. Conservatives who have more supporters of grammar schools in their midst were led by a Prime Minister who did not see a return to selection as the way forward for our education system. Michael Gove professed himself to be against further expansion of selective education. Labour, which harbours more anti-selection campaigners, was against any further expansion but would not take the decision to change the status of the 164 remaining grammar schools in the country. Enter Nicky Morgan who perhaps muddied the waters by giving the go-ahead for a satellite grammar school to the Weald of Kent Grammar School in Tonbridge to open seven miles down the road in Sevenoaks. The move to open the satellite came as a result of pressure from parents in Sevenoaks who claimed they were being discriminated against because they were the only ones in the county of Kent being denied the chance to send their children to a selective school because there was nothing available locally. In her granting of permission, Mrs Morgan insisted that the decision "does not reflect a change in this government's position on selective schools". It was, she argued, merely an expansion of an existing school and so therefore did not contravene legislation introduced under Labour forbidding the opening of new selective schools. Eyebrows perhaps could be raised about how far away a satellite school could be from its hub but if the government sticks to this policy it would appear that claims that this could open the floodgates to selection were wide of the mark – although there were a few areas of the country where a similar situation existed, most notably in Maidenhead (interestingly the constituency of our current Prime Minister Theresa May – a known supporter of grammar schools). In the meantime, some of the country's existing grammar schools were taking steps to improve the imbalance between the number of pupils on free school meals getting into grammar schools (three per cent of the intake) and the percentage in the country as a whole (15 per cent). Schools in Birmingham's King Edward VI Foundation – which includes five grammar schools – set themselves a target recruiting 20 per cent of pupils on free school meals. They did this by lowering the bar for entry (or pass mark in the 11-plus if you like) for pupils from disadvantaged backgrounds. Teachers from the schools also offered training to local primary schools to help their children cope with entrance tests. Given that we are unlikely to see an end to selective education, it seemed a welcome step towards creating a fairer admissions system for grammar schools. "The schools of King Edward don't need to do this," said Pete Slough, director of outreach for the foundation, said. "They have got 5,000 or 6,000 applicants for 600 places. We are doing it because it is the right thing that should be done." Other grammar schools around the country – including Kent, one of the few totally selective education areas of the country left, have expressed an interest in what Birmingham is doing with a view to following suit.

Selection and the desire to create a state education system where all schools are independently run represent two of the most constant themes for education debate during my 36 years of reporting – and it seems unlikely the arguments over these issues have as yet exhausted themselves. My advice to politicians would be: give us a break. It would appear that they are not listening, though. No sooner had Theresa May got her feet under the Downing Street table then she launched into a radical plan to bring back grammar schools. It came as a surprise. Critics of selection thought they had weathered 12 years of Thatcherism and four years of the radical right-wing reforms of Michael Gove without seeing a return to selection but it appeared that the 20 years of unofficial consensus over selection between the two major parties was over.

During her time in office, Mrs Morgan also demonstrated her enthusiasm for Lord Baker's University Technical Colleges – thought by many to be a far better way of improving the education on offer in the state sector. She promised legislation to ensure all schools give just as much weight to telling their pupils about vocational opportunities and apprenticeships as about university courses. This followed the revelation by Lord Baker that representatives of UTCs had been barred entry to existing secondary schools to speak to parents and pupils. The UTCs were, it was argued, at a disadvantage in recruitment as they offered the opportunity of a 14 to 19 education which meant they were trying to attract pupils at a time when they had already been in their existing secondary schools for two years. "It is a total hostility being shown by traditional education to something which is exciting and successful," said Lord Baker. "We can give them (the pupils) the skills that are right for the workplace."

It turned out to be one of Mrs Morgan's last acts as Education Secretary as she was one of those who fell victim to the arrival of Theresa May as Prime Minister in the aftermath of the EU referendum. Reasons for her dismissal were not clear – although she had supported Michael Gove, another casualty, in his (short-lived) campaign to become leader of the Conservative Party. Obviously, the next few years will be dominated by post-referendum issues but the new May administration did begin with one initiative which had the wholehearted support of almost everyone involved in education. It returned higher and further education from their slot within the Department for Business, Innovation and Skills to the Department for Education – thus seeming to confirm that, in the eyes of this new administration, universities and colleges were more about providing education than just preparing young people for the world of work.

There was also that second initiative – the return of grammar schools – that united much of the education world in horror at what the government was proposing.

Under Mrs May's plans, confirmed in a Green Paper published in September 2016, legislation banning the opening of more selective schools was to be repealed, every secondary school would be allowed to seek to take in some of their pupils through selection and – to try and ensure disadvantaged pupils were not excluded from the new grammar schools – there would be a quota on the number of deprived children taken in. This could be achieved through the Birmingham method of allowing a lower entry mark in the 11-plus for those from poorer homes.

For good measure, the Green Paper also gave the green light for faith schools to select all their pupils on the grounds of their religion. Mr Gove had introduced a new curb on free faith schools – only allowing them to select 50 per cent of pupils as a result of religious persuasion.

These reforms bore all the hallmarks of her senior adviser Nick Timothy, formerly chief executive of New Schools Network – the charity which helps free schools to establish themselves.

In an interview I did with him for *The Independent* about eight months before he changed jobs and swept into Downing Street alongside Mrs May, he was particularly concerned with the fact that the Roman Catholic Church was refusing to back free schools or set any up because of the restriction on taking in pupils of their faith. He was also a known supporter of the grammar school system.

Opposition to Mrs May's proposals was far and wide. From within the Conservative Party, there was David Willetts, the party's former education spokesman who had been reshuffled after a speech pointing out the pitfall of the grammar school system (that existing grammar schools took in few disadvantaged pupils – three per cent of their intake were on free school meals compared to 16 per cent in state schools at large), and Mrs Morgan who called the proposals "weird". One of the most forthright critics was Sir Michael Wilshaw, the chief schools inspector, who felt that creating new grammar schools would mean existing schools would no longer be able to take in the brightest 25 per cent of pupils in any given year group.

As a result, the ethos in these schools would be destroyed, their results in A-level and GCSE exams would plummet – all for the sake of giving just a handful of disadvantaged pupils a leg up out of their home circumstances. All the teachers' organisations expressed their horror at the proposals. Even Justine Greening, the new Education Secretary, came across as lukewarm about the proposals in interviews.

Rabbi Jonathan Romain, chairman of Accord, which seeks to put admissions to faith schools on the same footing as other schools, warned of increasing segregation if the cap on free school admissions was lifted. One Conservative MP was heard to mutter: "We'll be seeing a lot of madrasas opening up around the country."

Mrs May and her supporters countered by claiming they were offering parents more choice of schooling – a claim counteracted by her opponents who pointed out that in selective schools, the school chooses the children, not the other way.

It meant that, far from education taking a back seat on the political agenda, as had been expected following the aftermath of the pro-Brexit vote in the EU referendum, it was there in the centre stage once again. Some argued that may have been behind the proposal – the grammar school was a sop to the Conservative right, they argued, at a time when that section of the party was most likely to be critical if the government failed to deliver what it wanted following the Brexit vote. Whatever the rights and wrongs of the situation, it mean that battle between politicians and the profession over how state education should be run was continuing with a vengeance.

TIMELINE

2014

Nicky Morgan takes over as Education Secretary.

Teachers face disciplinary action if they allow pupils to be prey to extremist preachers, the government warns.

2015

Former Ofsted chief inspector Sir Chris Woodhead dies.

Government announces 500 more free schools in the lifetime of new Parliament.

2016

Government announces all schools will be forced to become academies by 2022.

Jeremy Corbyn becomes first party leader to address NUT conference.

Government forced to drop plan to make all schools become academies.

Epilogue

When I first started reporting on education, it was not just the national curriculum that was a secret garden. There was no compunction on schools to publish their exam results, all state schools were maintained by local education authorities, budgets were tightly controlled from the centre and schools often faced a morass of bureaucracy and delays as they tried to get the simplest things done. There was no Ofsted (some teachers might say this was a good thing) and – in general – there was little accountability in the education system.

The first senior politician who felt that things had to change was 1970s Prime Minister Jim Callaghan who – in his Ruskin College speech two years before leaving office – called for a "Great Debate" on education. That debate was meandering along its way as I took office with conferences arranged in local education authorities up and down the land. Change was slow in coming – it wasn't until the late 1980s that Mrs Thatcher really gave education reform top priority following the words she had spoken after years of bitter industrial battles with the teachers: "Something must be done about education". Her opponents would find those words quite chilling. The something that had to be done turned out to be the Great Education Reform Bill (GERBIL for short) ushered in by her then Education Secretary Kenneth (now Lord) Baker.

So, 36 years on, have things really changed and who is responsible for any improvements? Let's take a look at the men and women who were given responsibility for running our system first. It is difficult to give the 15 Secretaries of State I wrote about during my 36 years as an education correspondent a ranking order – but there are two I would pick out as having made the biggest contributions to the education system: one Conservative and one Labour. Step forward Kenneth Baker and David Blunkett. (Interestingly enough, when he was asked at a HMC conference two years ago – just before the General Election of 2015 – which Education Secretary he believed had made the greatest contribution, David Blunkett picked out Kenneth Baker, too.)

During his time at the helm the now Lord Baker was responsible for the introduction of the national curriculum – thus giving disadvantaged students a guarantee of the kind of education they should receive in schools; and the local management of schools – finally removing some of that needless bureaucracy faced by schools as they strove to get repairs done. He was also responsible for the introduction of City Technology Colleges. It might seem surprising that I should pick out that initiative. The government struggled to get enough sponsors to come forward to sponsor CTCs but it did lead to the creation of successful schools like Thomas Telford which became the first comprehensive school in the country to get 100 per cent of its pupils to obtain five top grade A* to C grade passes at GCSE. Okay, it might have done so by putting pupils in for vocational qualifications which – by some quirk of fate – were deemed the equivalent of four GCSE passes, but when the criteria for measuring schools changed to insist all pupils got top grade passes in maths and English it retained its position at the top of the league tables. No, the CTCs in themselves may not have been the success story of the era but they paved the way for – down the line – the University Technical College initiative which I believe is providing many 14 to 19-year-olds with the kind of skills qualifications they would need to succeed in the world of work. In essence, they were organised along the lines of the German education system – which has long been recognised as a leading light in the provision of vocational education. The UTC project is coupled with a separate drive to persuade existing further education colleges to embrace Lord Baker's careers college initiative – where teenagers can find the training to succeed in a particular career. One of the best examples of this I saw came with a visit to the Air and Defence Career College in Lincoln where young people are offered a range of training which would help them take up posts in the RAF. They don't have to – the kind of training they receive would equip them for a range of engineering jobs, too, but the area of Lincolnshire it operates in does offer a range of employment opportunities in the RAF. One flaw in the UTC system is the difficulty it faces recruiting students at the age of 14 – two years after they will have started in a mainstream secondary school. This needs to be addressed by promised legislation giving the UTCs the right to enter mainstream schools to talk about what they have to offer.

As for David Blunkett, the greatest reform he introduced was the moves he made towards improving reading and numeracy standards in primary schools. According to the highly respected National Foundation for Education Research, reading standards – in particular – in schools had stagnated since the Second World War. With his introduction of the literacy hour and daily maths lesson in schools, he masterminded the first real improvement in standards for more than 50 years. It was ironic that this was one of the issues that brought his successor, Estelle (now Baroness) Morris down because the government failed to reach in 2002 ambitious targets it had set in 1997. It had improved the standard of education, though. Nobody could deny that (although to look at the hymn sheet from the Gove era you might think Mr Blunkett had sat on his backside and done absolutely nothing to improve standards in the three Rs). I think Mr Blunkett could also take credit for changing the climate of opinion within the education world – and instilling a belief that poverty is no reason for failure. He did that through a string of initiatives – including setting targets for GCSE results, and the "fresh start" for failing schools whereby the name of the school was changed and a new leadership team installed. He also created a climate whereby the business world appeared more responsive towards sponsoring schools than had been the case at the time of Lord Baker's CTC initiative. More money was ploughed into education, too – leading to a marked increase in the repairs and building programme. The idea was that, if you gave pupils decent conditions in which to learn, it showed them how much you valued giving them a decent education (and how much respect you had for them).

Moving on, though, if there was an Oscar to be awarded for the best education team, I think it would have to go to the regime that was set up under Charles Clarke's reign. He had Alan Johnson as his Higher Education Minister and inherited David Miliband as his Schools Minister. I have told you the joke Alan Johnson told about the way he and Mr Clarke approached the introduction of top-up fees. They launched a "charm offensive" – "I was charming and Charles was offensive". Actually, the approach was a bit more nuanced than that. Mr Clarke was firm in spelling out the options available to backbench Labour MPs reluctant to support a rise in student fees: no expansion of higher education without it. Tony Blair had talked about wanting to increase the participation rate in higher education to 50 per cent – but who was going to pay for that? The only way to finance it, argued Mr Clarke, was to find more of a contribution from students. In the end, with a healthy dollop of support for disadvantaged students in terms of maintenance grants, he managed to secure enough support to get the package through the Commons by five votes. Meanwhile, David Miliband was given the task of taking charge of the Tomlinson inquiry into exam reform. He did a sterling job in managing to secure backing for its recommendations – the main one of which was the overarching diplomas covering GCSE and A-levels and vocational qualifications – from all the teachers' and heads' organisations and the CBI. Sadly, at the end of the day he failed to convince the one man who mattered – Mr Blair – and the proposal fell by the wayside amidst images of headlines in the Daily Mail about Labour destroying the "Gold Standard" of the education system during an election campaign. If Mr Miliband had managed to get the support of Number 10, that administration could have gone down as one of the most reforming education administrations in history. Sadly, it did not – though not as a result of any lack of effort on the part of its three main protagonists.

And now the one that you have all been waiting for – if I am going to issue plaudits for the best performing Education Secretaries of my time, I have to single out the worst as well. Talking to people involved in the education world, most are agreed on this – it was John Patten. Some say Michael Gove but that is on ideological grounds, not competence in office. No, the gaffe-prone Mr Patten holds sway for promising to eat his hat if the government failed to persuade a majority of schools to opt out of local education authority control, turning a press launch over discipline policy into a farce by reminiscing about how he had been flogged by monks at school, and failing to deliver on introducing what was termed a "Mum's Army" into schools – untrained staff to work alongside teachers – because of opposition from the unions. For good measure, he also turned down the opportunity to speak at a number of key education conferences, citing pressure of work – although on one occasion he was found lunching with a journalist instead. However, I should add that I don't think he should march alone into the Room 101 for Education Secretaries.

I would have to add that I don't think Labour's Ruth Kelly covered herself with glory in the post either. As an education correspondent, you get a feeling for the confidence of an Education Secretary. On one occasion, after she had made what was intended as a keynote speech to the North of England Education Conference, she was going by lift to a room where she could relax. It was almost empty when it stopped at a floor where I was one of three journalists wanting to get in. One of her civil servants made a great fuss about how the lift was not open to the press. One of my colleagues pointed out it was a public lift owned by the university where the conference was being held. Personally I could not care whether I got in the lift with her or not but as I saw her cowering in the corner, refraining from speaking – obviously wishing the press had not disturbed her – I formed the impression that she was just not happy defending her brief. She got moved on from the post by Tony Blair because she failed to persuade Labour MPs of his vision that every state school should be a self-governing school. I have more sympathy with her on this. It was not an easy task. I must say, though, it is difficult to think of a lasting legacy that she has left the education system with.

As for the others I have had to deal with, when I started on the national beat Mark Carlisle was the first Secretary of State I came across. "Mark who?" is the response of many people asked to remember him nowadays. The reason he remains in relative obscurity is probably more as a result of the incoming Thatcher government not making education one of its first priorities as it set about its business. One thing that does stand out from his time, though, is how he presided over dropping a plan to set targets as to how much time should be spent on core subjects like maths, English and science in the curriculum. It was dropped, we were told, because "nobody seemed to like it". Bizarre reasoning. That would not have happened with some of the latter day politicos who took over his office. In fact, in at least a couple of cases, that would have been a positive spur in wanting to go ahead with the plan.

He was followed by Sir Keith Joseph and I have to say I doubt if any holder of his office – to use a phrase that he constantly used to describe himself, often provoking a flurry of speculation that he was about to leave – has had more integrity than he had. Unfortunately, though, he would agonise over his brief before reaching a decision – thus often clogging up the wheels of progress. Also he was loath to part from his monetarist soul, so negotiating with teachers' leaders at a time of constant industrial action was not a strength of his as he could not bear the thought of adding more money to the education system. Witness the agonising 50-second silence after he was asked by the BBC whether teachers were well paid if you want an example of his dithering. He never answered the question.

Kenneth Baker, whom we have already dealt with, followed him into office as the Thatcher government got to grips with education reform. After the fanfare of the GERBIL, it needed a quieter soul to adopt a "steady as she goes" approach to education. Step forward John McGregor. It seems in the annals of education history that there is an ebb and flow to politics – and a reforming zealot is often replaced by someone with quieter instincts. It happened again with Nicky Morgan when she replaced Michael Gove. Both were competent in that role – although Mrs Morgan courted more controversy after she embraced David Cameron's call for every state school to become an academy. She also fell into the ranks of those that I considered not to be confident in her brief. Witness an address she was to give to a conference at the leading independent school, Brighton College, the day before George Osborne was due to announce his Budget. She cut the speech down from an hour to 10 minutes, refused to take any questions and then beetled off to a classroom to see some children learning Mandarin, barring the press from the room despite the school's head, Richard Cairns, wanting them to attend. It was said that they were worried she might say something out of turn on what was to be Mr Osborne's big day. Oh, please! Just don't say anything stupid, Nicky, if you can manage that. However, I do have to praise her for the settlement that she won for education in this year's budget which saw the pledge to maintain education spending increased to cover sixth-form spending for the first time. This followed a highly effective campaign on the impact of cuts (and having to make VAT payments which the Chancellor also dealt with) by the Sixth Form Colleges Association. So not Room 101 for her – or John MacGregor who was in office for such a short time; it is hard to give him a rating.

We then come to the highly competent ministers who went about their business without a fuss. I would put Gillian Shephard and Alan Johnson in this category. Neither went looking for headline-grabbing initiatives, both gained the respect of the profession. In Mrs Shephard's case there were disagreements with her party leader (John Major) especially over the idea of creating a grammar school in every town promoted by him. Mr Johnson was moved up the chain to the Home Office after Gordon Brown took over as Prime Minister following a series of modest reforms – including pressing ahead with the idea of raising the education leaving age to 18 to try and rid the UK of its woeful record in persuading teenagers to carry on in the classroom or training.

And then there were four. Kenneth Clarke was sent in to replace John MacGregor to carry on with implementing and embellishing Kenneth Baker's reforms. He had the image in the eyes of the public at large of being a blokey, Liberal-minded Conservative that people felt they could do business with. Unfortunately, that image never really rubbed off on the education profession and comments like this one, made in a magazine interview, did not help – "I have never met anyone who did not want to send their children into independent education if they could afford it". Not really the type of response that would go down well with state school employees. He also poured cold water on the idea of expanding nursery education, saying of a pledge – that all three and four-year-olds should have a nursery place – made by Mrs Thatcher when she was Education Secretary in 1971 that it was "not a promise anybody can sensibly renew". As a result, when he was replaced after the 1992 election there was no great sadness that he was moving on.

Estelle Morris, who took over from David Blunkett after the 2001 election, was probably the one that could most accurately be labelled "the teachers' friend". She had been a comprehensive school teacher herself and was also educated in a comprehensive school. She was also the only one of the 15 Education Secretaries I have reported on to have considered herself not up to the job. Many people would have preferred it if others had come to that conclusion. She was the only one to resign (rather than be reshuffled or moved out of office) – largely as a result of a pledge made in the infancy of the Labour years to resign if ambitious targets for improving literacy and numeracy standards were not met. As mentioned before, they were not met but there was an improvement in standards. Sources within Labour did not think it was a resigning issue – but Ms Morris was finding it difficult to cope with the constant scrutiny and prying into her private life. She also had misgivings about the next item on her agenda – introducing top-up fees. (This was before higher education was palmed off to the Department for Business, Innovation and Skills.) After she left, she kept in touch with the education world, becoming a university chancellor and giving speeches on the subject. It would be true to say that she was still held in affection and high esteem by those in education who had worked with her years after she left.

Ed Balls, who replaced Alan Johnson when Gordon Brown became Prime Minister, tried to put his stamp on the education world. He was in fact one of the longer-serving Education Secretaries. He was keen on boosting languages in secondary schools – particularly those that were becoming more important in the modern business world like Mandarin. He also tried to put Labour's version of the Tomlinson diploma on the map. It was a separate qualification offered as an alternative to GCSEs and A-level but – as such – fell at the perennial hurdle of being considered a second-class qualification which Tomlinson's idea of an overarching diploma covering both the academic and vocational areas would hopefully have overcome. He said that he felt it would in future be considered the natural route of progression for sixth-formers rather than A-levels but figures showing take-up constantly disproved this theory. What Labour would have done with the exam system if it had been returned to office in 2010, one can only speculate. There was serious thinking within the party when in opposition that it would finally embrace the Tomlinson proposals. We shall never know, though.

And finally: Michael Gove. No one could deny that he deserved an A for effort in his attempt to radically reform the education system. The trouble is, he felt he could do it without the support of the teaching profession or indeed anyone outside a small coterie of admirers. He had some good ideas. The English Baccalaureate (measuring schools' attainment) was superficially an attractive idea. It did lead to a take-up in foreign languages (initially) and science subjects in schools – something very much needed. However, it also led to a drop in the pass rate in some key academic subject areas – possibly because schools had put some pupils in for its subjects who were finding it too hard to manage. It was also much narrower in its base than the International Baccalaureate: the arts were not included in it, nor were religious education or, initially, technology – although this eventually squeezed in as a science subject. If there is one main criticism of his performance, it is that he appeared not to see the value of anyone gaining skills qualifications – believing an academic education was all you should aspire to. Fair play, access to an academic education for disadvantaged pupils needed to be widened – but not everyone can benefit from that route through education.

Then there was the free schools and academies programme. I could see an attraction in the free schools programme if it was providing an alternative education that was not catered for by the state sector – such as the two free schools who were providing bilingual primary schools, one German/English and the other Spanish/English. I was also persuaded to support a free school application which would have provided a predominantly black pupil intake with the guarantee of three months' work experience immediately on leaving school and held out aspirations for its pupils to get into Oxbridge. What I could not stomach was the kind of John Wayne approach that Mr Gove and his advisers had to education provision. You remember the lines from old films: "the only good Indian is a dead Indian." I seem to remember some of John Wayne's characters having the same thoughts about Communists, too. Well, Mr Gove's approach appeared to me: "The only good local authority school is an ex-local authority school." Some schools, I have to admit, shone under the academies programme and the free school initiative. Others, though, failed. The truth is there are good local authority schools, good free schools and good academies but there are also bad local authority schools, bad free schools and bad academies and the sooner we got some more honesty into this debate the better. Politicians should realise that one-size-fits-all – the very phrase used to criticise the comprehensive system – is not an appropriate way forward.

A final word, though, on the influence of politics in education. It will not be that easy, given the stances of the two main political parties. I can recall at that conference where David Blunkett selected Kenneth Baker as his nominee for best Education Secretary that he was also asked whether the impending election campaign (this was October 2014) would be divisive. He said there would probably be a lot of hot air but that – on analysis – the direction of travel between the two parties was not as different as was often made out. After all, who started the academies programme? Labour. He did not say this but it is also fair to point out that both Tony Blair and David Cameron wanted every state school to become a self-governing school along the lines of those in the independent sector. In view of the many critical reports about how academy chains are operating, I am tempted to say 'so much for evidence based politics'.

*****

That's it for the politicians, then, but what about their policies? Which have been the most successful and which have had the most impact on the education system?

I have to tell you that the policy I would choose as having had the most beneficial impact on the education system was not one rushed through the Commons with zeal by the politicians. It was the abolition of corporal punishment – the UK became a society where we no longer sanctioned the beating of children. It almost scraped through the House of Commons by default – the then Thatcher government did not want to introduce it but most sane observers realised that after a European Court ruling that parents had the right to declare that their children should not be beaten at school it made no sense to keep it as a deterrent. After all, how could you have two pupils guilty of the same crime – one of whom could be beaten for it and the other not? Common sense did prevail, though, and – though we were one of the last countries in Europe to abolish it – we eventually bit the bullet and did so.

What other reforms, then, have had a major impact? The improvement in literacy and numeracy standards through the introduction of the literacy hour and the daily maths lesson; the stress by both Labour and Conservative governments that disadvantage should be no excuse for failure has led to a more "can do" approach in a number of inner city schools in particular. Then there was the introduction of the national curriculum – giving every pupil an entitlement to what they should be learning at school for the first time. I also believe you need an organisation like Ofsted to monitor the education system – although I would admit there is sometimes an imbalance between criticism and praise in their judgements. Many people point out that Ofsted's job stops at pointing out faults – unlike its predecessor HMI it does not work with schools to provide a solution to their problems. Reducing class sizes to thirty for five to seven-year-olds as introduced by the Blair government in 1997 also deserves praise. Would that it had been built upon, though. Local financial management of schools has also had a tremendously beneficial impact on the system, giving headteachers more say in the way they run their schools. I would stop there but add a rider that the academies drive – because of the compulsion that has been applied and the denigration of the local authority sector that has often accompanied it – cannot be greeted with universal delight. Indeed, just the reverse in some cases. Take the case of Harrowden Middle School in Bedford.

The school won plaudits from Ofsted as "good" and its headteacher Deirdre Murphy was praised for her "outstanding commitment". There was an upper school nearby which was struggling and therefore compelled to become an academy with a cash injection of £22.5 million from the government. The nearest lower school had also been placed in special measures by Ofsted and had no track record of preparing children for national curriculum tests at 11 since it only took pupils up to the age of eight. When it came to reorganisation, which of these three schools was earmarked for closure? Answer: Harrowden. With the upper school, which lowered its starting age to 11 to compete with Harrowden for pupils, Bedford had no jurisdiction over it and could not recommend it for closure. There was a feeling, too, in government circles that as £22.5 million had been invested in it, it should be kept open. Ironically, Harrowden was in line for its next Ofsted inspection as it faced closure. The report was published just a few days before its demise. What did it say of the school? "The school is a happy, caring community where the pupils thrive," it said. Not any more. It's gone and it is decisions like this that make you realise the simple mantra of "local authority schools – bad, academies – good" is senseless.

Going on to free schools, I would take exception to the idea that every new school has to be a free school – especially at a time of rising pupil numbers. I accept that the majority of free schools have been opened in areas of need but the plain truth is you cannot guarantee that a private sponsor, chain or – far more rarely these days – group of parents will come up with a proposal to open a free school in every area where there is need. Local education authorities still have the obligation to ensure provision of a school place for every child who is eligible for one and the only way they can ensure this is by persuading existing schools to expand. Sometimes this has meant creating extra classrooms out of space dedicated for school libraries or arts provision – and that cannot be right. Most parties talk ad nauseam about providing parental choice but that seems meaningless if you only allow new schools to be free schools.

In higher education, the fees policy does not seem to have had that much of an impact on demand for places. Indeed, the numbers applying from disadvantaged backgrounds has increased since the introduction of the £9,000 tuition fees – mainly as a result of the fact that students do not have to pay anything up front or start repaying until they are earning £21,000 a year. That, though, appears to be storing up trouble for the future as the estimates are that the majority of graduates will end up having at least part of their debt written off – with the result that the new system may end up costing the taxpayer more than the one in place before fees were introduced.

I would also like to see the debate over grammar schools and selection dead and buried once and for all. Let's face it: the age of 11 is too young to divide children into sheep and goats and I would like the supporters of grammar schools to be a bit more honest about their desire to bring back secondary modern schools for the majority of the population. I would like to see it dead and buried but that may be one thing on my bucket list that I never achieve if Theresa May's determination is anything to go by, Her proposals risk undoing any of the good that was created by academies and free schools and the successful drive to improve standards in London's state schools.

So what would I like to see done to improve the education system? Well, I would like an increase in the provision of University Technical Colleges, a guarantee that they are put on an equal footing with mainstream secondary schools when it comes to telling parents and pupils what choices are on offer to them. I still think that the Tomlinson inquiry reforms – with their overarching diploma – offer the best way forward for 14 to 19 education and I would like to see an extension of the English Baccalaureate so it becomes as broad in its curriculum as the IB (although I accept that by changing performance tables so they now measure a pupil's GCSE performance on their achievements in their best eight subjects has gone a long way towards achieving this). This probably does not come within the remit of this book but I would also like to see more evidence of mergers or getting-togethers between the various teachers' organisations so that the profession may be able to speak with one voice. That is why I am pleased at the efforts being made by the NUT and ATL to get together. You can never ask for a moratorium on education reform – because events may conspire against you – but I would like to see less zeal from politicians for reforming the education system just to look as though they are being active. The trouble is that, in order to make their case for change, they start denigrating the existing system, as a result damaging morale in the state sector. A prime example of this was Michael Gove's zeal for reforming the examination system which meant decrying existing A-levels and GCSEs at a time when pupils were sitting their exams. Think, I would urge politicians, about the impact your words can have before you utter them.

During my lifetime as an education correspondent, there are two reforms which have cropped up from time to time that I would like to see implemented. I have lost count of the number of times that reports have been commissioned investigating whether the traditional three-term year for schools should be replaced by a four, five or even six-term year. All have agreed that it should. Local education authorities have unanimously backed the idea. The essence of the change is to limit the amount of time the pupil is out of school during the summer holidays. With the current system, much of the first few weeks of the autumn term is used up by helping the pupil to remember what they had learnt in the summer term – recapping instead of moving forward. Teachers' organisations have always fought this suggestion – claiming that their members need that long summer break to recover from the school year. (They add that it is not all holiday as they have to prepare for the next academic year.) Nigel de Gruchy, I seem to recall, called it "the last perk of the teaching profession" and threatened industrial action were it ever to be recommended it should go. My point is this: teachers would still work exactly the same number of days in school under any shake-up and they may be less stressed coming up to a break if the term has not been so long. It could be win-win for both pupils and teachers.

Reform number two is grandly titled PQA (Post-Qualification Application). It means applying for your university place after you have got your A-level results and not before. It would replace the current situation where students are offered places on predicted grades (which can often be wrong). It is felt in many circles that the current system favours the privileged as disadvantaged students lack the confidence to apply for places at the country's more selective universities until they have their A-level grades in the bag. That is one advantage such a change would have – a change that, again, has been recommended by many commissions and inquiries held into the subject and at one time was backed by Charles Clarke when he was Education Secretary. The other advantage is that it is logical – try explaining the current system to a Martian and you'll understand that! Trouble is, it would need flexibility on the part of the exam boards and the universities to create the time to enable it to happen (not that much now online marking can reduce the time between taking an exam and getting your results). Neither have been prepared to play ball with this, though, and so the inquiries gather dust at the back of university libraries and we struggle on with the current imperfect system (which has been rendered more imperfect, according to Cambridge University, by the government's decision to uncouple AS-levels from A-levels – with the result that fewer students are taking them and universities have even less evidence of what a pupil can achieve at sixth-form before having to decide whether to offer a place).

I had hoped that both these reforms would be in place by the time I hung up my boots, but sadly they are not and I doubt whether I could promise any successors that I have that they would be able to preside over their introduction either. That's it then. I think we have a better system in place 36 years after I first started surveying the education scene – so therefore I would have to agree some form of government intervention has been necessary. Just beware the over-zealous politician anxious to make a mark, though.

If I had to bestow a lifetime achievement award (which they do in the annual

Teaching Awards and which I myself received eight years into the annual education awards – making me realise for the first time that some people perhaps thought it was about time I should consider retiring!), I would have to award it to the teaching profession for having got on with the job while all around was changing. In making this award, I would give a special mention to those headteachers who – when receiving the latest set of guidance, advice and instructions from the Department for Education or whatever its predecessor's names were – filed it in the bin and carried on with what they had been doing successfully up until that time.

MY WISH LIST

2017

Government implements four-term year.

Sir Mike Tomlinson asked to revise his inquiry into exam reform.

2018

Government accepts case for overarching diploma.

Fifty new University Technical Colleges announced.

2019

Universities and exam boards come up with joint initiative to introduce Post-Qualification Application.

2020

Government goes into next election with pledge to allow education reforms to bed down before further change.